All the Women Were Heroes

brainchild writers
of springfield

ROSEHILL PRESS
Springfield, Illinois

Publication of Brainchild's 25th anniversary anthology was supported in part by a grant from the Springfield Area Arts Council, the Illinois Arts Council and First National Bank, and by contributions from Friends of Brainchild.

Copyright © 1997 by Brainchild Writers of Springfield
All rights reserved.

Some of the stories and poems in this anthology have been previously published, and we would like to acknowledge their sources. "Saab Story," "Time," "The Pause in Between" and "Bad Blood" appeared in *Rosie: Selected Works by Rosemary Richmond*. "Garden of the Hungry Cats" by Martha Miller was originally published in *Common Lives/Lesbian Lives*. "An Unsent Letter" by Martha Miller appeared in *Lesbians Raising Sons*. "Alberta Lived To Be Ninety-Three" by Jane Morrel is taken from her book *This Paradox Shadow*.

Rosehill Press
545 S. Feldkamp Ave.
Springfield, IL 62704
(217) 793-2587

Library of Congress Catalog Card No.: 97-69300
ISBN: 0-9646037-6-4

Manufactured in the U.S.A. on recycled paper using soy inks

To Rosemary Richmond

On my shelf reserved for children
there's a magic lens for seeing
anything,
multiplied,
rotate around center.

Rosie was like that,
acting as a lens,
helping us to see.

She was a woman
multifaceted
reflecting quality, elegance
yet more ... a loving heart.

Martha McGill

And her sisters in spirit

Brainchild is a blueberry bush.
Stories fall in clumps, like berries,
some luscious, some not quite ready,
waiting for sun and time to ripen them.

Like berries, stories need nurturance.
Brainchild is the irrigation, the water.
I relish these morsels, gobble them up,
the sweet and the bitter.

Rosemary Richmond

Contents

Acknowledgements viii
Letter from Brainchild 1

Jacqueline Jackson
    Paradise (From *The Round Barn*)   5
    The Great Hayloft in the Sky (From *The Round Barn*)   9
    Poem   11

Deborah Brothers
    Excerpt from *Sidewinder*   13
    Leather Peace Ring   16

Pat Martin
    1948: Taylorville, Illinois   20
    Grandma's Story: "I Never Knew"   21
    Taproot   22
    Little Red Car   23
    Strangely Comforted   24
    Ambushed   25
    Warm Satin Milk   26
    I Don't Belong   27
    Trailing Enough Remembering   28
    The Prophet's Touch   29

Carol Manley
    Gramma and the Butcher   30
    Nine and a Half Months   34

Nancy Pistorius
    Reminders   38
    quickenings   39

waiting room   40
to my husband, sleeping, in winter   41
who gets the chicken heart?   42
birthday blues   43
single exposure   44
Sorry, Emily   44

Sue Daugherty
For a daughter, nearly grown   45
Did he hurt you?   47
A Requiem for Red   49

Martha Miller
An Unsent Letter   51
Garden of the Hungry Cats   57

Maria Mootry
He's driving around town in her car   59
Looking for Langston   62
Looking for Langston in Lincoln, Illinois   63
Langston at Dakar: Presence Africaine   64
In a Dialogic Mode (Deloria & Friends Talk)   65
At the Kitchen Table, My Aunt Jean Confesses   66
Ginny Lee, Photographer   67
To Gwen, Painter of Words   67
The Rest of the Story   68

Peg Knoepfle
O Deer   69
Letter to My Daughter   71
Position Title: Clerk Typist II   73

Rosemary Richmond
Saab Story   75
The Pause in Between   78
Time   78
Bad Blood   79

Vicki Bamman
I don't understand why we're friends   80
The Interview   82
Rage   82
The flowers on my desk are dying   83
Can you hear me?   84
The merry-go-round   85

Debi Sue Edmund
Back Talk   86

Kate Kanaley Miller
this is the first tree   91
back to the tree   92
without walking   92
it's that uncluttered look I want   93
at the bookstore weeping words   94
Jesus coming to you altared   96
your eagerness to hear me   97
in-corporate   97
that's all you have to do   98
to Anne Frank   99

Hilda Beltran Wagner
How He Made Do   100

Rena Brannan
Monochrome   102

Tavia Ervin
The Pastor's Wife   107

Martha McGill
On Writing   116
Old Photographs: 1860-1900   117
Blow me a shape   118
from its waters we all rise   118
We were summer's children   119
and here i am   120
Look at me   121
All she could do was look at us   121
Across the pasture   121
outrageous!!   122
Hairpeace   123

Becky Bradway
Excerpt from *Searching for the Muses*   125

Sue Sitki
Undernight   130

Bonnie Madison
Big   138

Bypassing Toronto   139
Visit to a Country Home   140
Gladys   141
Amputee   141
Knitting   142
Memorial Garden 6/87 For Brother   142
The Party   143

Debra Nickelson Smith
The Deal (From *The Long Sneak*)   148

Roberta DeKay
And Another Woman Leaves Ireland   153
Belief and the Blooming Jacaranda Trees   155
Sonya Tolstoy   156
Something Holy   157

Linda McElroy
Flight to Freeport   158

Gael Carnes
Novel Excerpt   161

Jane Morrel
Alberta Lived To Be Ninety-Three   171

Celia Wesle
From the Train Window   173
The Painting   174
Walk to School   175
Lovely   176
From the Porch Swing   177
The Decades   178
I Hear Her   178
Spiritual Rejuvenation   179
Weaving   180
The Bath   182

Sandra Olivetti Martin
A Hero Among Women (For Rosie)   183

***Voices*, by Pat Martin   193**
About the Authors   194
***Afterword*, by Kate Kanaley Miller   200**

Acknowledgements

Without the help of good friends who made special contributions above the price of a book purchase, *All the Women Were Heroes* could not have been published. Brainchild would like to thank the following generous sponsors:

Ricardo Amézquita
Rose Corgan
Lynda Dautenhahn and Lee Nickelson
J.M. Desper
Janice DiGirolamo
Lori Dodwell
John Knoepfle
Elinor Petusky
Polly Poskin
Bev Rulon
Lynette Seator
Christopher Smith
Rebecca Winning

We would also like to thank Rosemary Richmond's daughter, Stacia Stinnett, and Jane Morrel's daughter, Corlyss Disbrow, for granting us permission to publish their mothers' work in this anthology.

In addition, we are grateful to those organizations (especially the Springfield Area Arts Council) which have invited us to perform over the years, the friends and relatives who have attended our performances, and the teachers (especially John Knoepfle and Jackie Jackson) who have nurtured and encouraged our writing.

All these people have played a vital role in helping us get our work out of dresser drawers and filing cabinets, and before the public.

Letter from Brainchild

In August 1972, a small group of women gathered in the living room of Sandra Martin's house at 1004 North Sixth Street. While sipping Pat Smith's hot buttered rum, the women discovered something in common — the unpublished poems and stories sitting in the bottoms of filing cabinets and dresser drawers. Peg Knoepfle had a suggestion. Why not create a writers' group?

"Peg in effect invited us out of the closet, saying we might as well call ourselves writers, since enough time was passing to make it clear that nobody else was going to," Sandra says. "Hands and voices shook as we read, and the thing I remember most was how good everybody sounded to everybody else. That little moment of assent, the sisterhood's pronouncement that I had words and they were good, gave me my voice."

Thus *brainchild* was born (in the old days we spelled it lowercase), along with a twofold mission that survives to this day: to encourage women's literary expression and to provide a public forum for our work.

Encouraging women's literary expression was a radical idea to many of us, at least in the early seventies. "The only woman author I remember reading in high school was George Eliot," says current Brainchild member Carol Manley. "That was a powerful message — if you're a woman who wants to write, do it in disguise."

"I had come up through a 1950s academic poetry background," Peg says. "A certain kind of writing was looked down on because it was 'personal.' It dealt with 'embarrassing things.' These seemed to include experiences unique to women, especially physical experiences like menstruation, pregnancy, childbirth. This kind of writing was considered coy. Narcissistic. Self-indulgent."

As we listened to each other's poems and stories, we noticed we began to write differently ourselves. "What we felt and what we said, what we read and what we wrote was vastly different from what we had done in university workshops," Peg relates. "Something had changed radically the minute we were all women together in a room."

We wrote about our daily lives: dirty laundry, child-rearing, relationships. We wrote about social issues, and the world that was suddenly expanding for us: feminism, women in the workplace, picket lines, atomic bombs, the environment, spirituality. Some of us even grew brave enough to write about things people weren't talking about: domestic violence, child abuse, rape and incest, erotic love, including lesbian love, and rage.

Our expression took on a variety of forms — novels and short stories, poetry, essays, articles and journal entries. In a culture that gave us mostly male icons, we created heroes of our own — our sisters, our mothers, our grandmothers, our daughters, our girlfriends. "We were writing about our lives changing," says Peg. "And what we wrote changed our lives."

But we also needed the encouragement that comes from presenting our stories and poems to an audience outside our group. Hence Brainchild's other purpose: to create a public forum for our work. "It was a way of asserting ourselves, of saying, 'We are writers,'" Peg says.

Some performances have become the stuff of legend. One famous (or infamous) example was Jackie Jackson's poem about vaginal itch, which premiered at a 1973 public reading. "That poem was awesome," Rosie Richmond once said, when explaining what inspired her to join Brainchild. Rosie wrote some outrageous — and pioneering — things of her own about topics ranging from being broke and gaining weight to menopause and sexual fantasies.

Jane Morrel, who was having a poetic renaissance at the age of 72 and whose spirit inspired us in those early years, made us cry with poems like "Alberta Lived To Be Ninety-Three."

When conventional forms of writing failed to convey our experience, we invented new forms. Jackie Jackson's *The Round Barn* is part fiction, part history — personal history, family history, community history. Recently, the story has stepped out of her book. Publicity about the upcoming publication of the book is helping make it possible to save the barn that was the center of her family farm.

In its quarter century of existence, our constantly-changing yet remarkably stable group has included members with a variety of backgrounds and levels of experience as writers. We have made a point of keeping our membership open to beginning as well as published authors. Those who have graduated from formal university writing programs find that our group gives them the needed support to keep writing, while some who joined our group as beginners have gone on to pursue formal writing courses.

Members agree that one of our greatest strengths lies in our diversity. In any group of writers, one would expect to find the journalists and English teachers, and we have those. We have also been hairdressers, counselors, secretaries, craftspeople, waitresses, foster parents, farmworkers, a minister, even a blackjack dealer. We have been white, Latina, African American, Native American, Asian American. We have been straight, lesbian, Catholic, Protestant, Jewish, Pagan, ages eighteen to seventy-two.

Some new members hear about Brainchild through friends. Librarians have referred others to our group. Still more have come to us via creative writing classes taught by Jackie Jackson or John Knoepfle at Sangamon State University (now the University of Illinois at Springfield). Many of us have reported feeling downright scared when we came to our first meeting.

The camaraderie almost immediately puts new members at ease. "Some part of my brain couldn't connect the fantasy life of The Writer with the work I did putting wheels on lawnmowers and envelopes in boxes," says Carol Manley. "I certainly could not be a writer. Then I met Jackie Jackson . . . and then Peg, and Celia . . . it finally began to penetrate my consciousness that I didn't have to be Norman Mailer

This photo of early Brainchild members appeared on the cover of our fourth anthology in 1977. Top row, left to right: Susan Sherard, Charlotte Napier Proctor, Peg Knoepfle, Margaret Hilligoss, Nancy Lee Hayes, Kathy Wood, Rose Wohl, Debrah Levenson, Roberta DeKay and Judi Scott. Sitting: Lynn Novotnak, Carla Cravens, Rosie Richmond, Mary Anne Demas, Katherine Lawson and Susan Luck. (Haven't changed a bit, have we?)

to write. The message of Brainchild is that all you have to do to be a writer, is write."

"Brainchild has provided an invaluable training ground and a comfort zone for me," says Maria Mootry. "My poems and a nascent novel have been gently critiqued in a cozy atmosphere with shared banana bread, Brie and iced tea. Little reminiscences, shared milestones, respect for ideas, and ways of expressing those ideas."

Indeed, food and friendship have been every bit as meaningful a part of Brainchild as the writing and performing. Rena Brannan, a member during the 1980s now living in England, recalls the magic of meetings in Rosie Richmond's third floor apartment: "Coke with a few ice cubes. Popcorn in a big green bowl. Oil hanging in the air. So many words. So many words. I sat at that table round and plump from the power of some of the greatest writers on this planet. More admirable than Dorothy Parker's roundtable."

Over the years, Brainchild has grown, both in size and reputation. We've now published seven anthologies, including one that featured a collection of dramatic narratives performed by actors onstage. Members who came to the group as beginners have gone on to be widely published, and have reaped numerous literary grants and awards. In 1995, Brainchild members swept all three of Lincoln Library's Writer of the Year awards: fiction, nonfiction and poetry.

No one could have predicted the power of a group consisting of so many different voices — it became much more than the individual writer making her voice heard. This newfound power has taken us where we never dreamed of going. Brainchild has become a fixture at Springfield's annual FirstNight celebration of the arts. We've been invited to read at Take Back the Night rallies and healing ceremonies. We've read to an audience in the town square that included homeless people, and our performances have helped raise money for a battered women's shelter. In short, we've become not just a group of writers, but a respected community arts organization.

Meanwhile Brainchild continues to be what it always has been — in current member Sue Sitki's words — "a haven for wise, wayward, wistful, weird, wandering, wonderful, writing women in all sizes, shapes, colors and years."

With this latest anthology, *All the Women Were Heroes,* Brainchild celebrates twenty-five years of encouraging women's literary expression. We hope you will like reading these poems and stories as much as we've enjoyed sharing them.

Jacqueline Jackson

◆

Paradise (From *The Round Barn*)

Joan, Patsy, Jackie and Craig know what Paradise is. They have dwelt there. It's the room over the milk house.

When the milk house was first built, that space was a bunkhouse for the hired men. After the Big House had its roof raised and dormitory rooms put in, the bunkhouse became an apartment for a succession of married couples. One of these was Lester and Moo Moo Stam, who moved out in the middle of the night after Moo Moo and Grama had a fight over nobody ever knew what. It has been empty now for quite some time.

There are really several rooms, each commanding a view over a portion of the farm, so that a trip through the apartment lets you see from on high everything that is going on. The floors are broad golden planks, and the walls and ceilings are painted white. It's a fresh and sunny place, with built-in cabinets and large drawers forming one whole wall of the largest room. It is this room that turns into Paradise.

It happens this way. The rich relatives that live in Elgin have bought new furniture. They offer to sell Daddy and Mother their old furniture at a very low price. Old Bosworth furniture is much finer than anything Mother and Daddy now have.

Mother and Daddy drive a truck down to Elgin to look over the discards and pick out what they want. They return with a bird's-eye maple bedroom suite, a dining room table and eight chairs, several marble-topped bedroom tables, an ornate four-sided pivoting bookcase, and other assorted pieces. Aside from trying out the spin on the bookcase, the four children are not particularly interested in the spoils.

But then Daddy says, "They threw in something for you. Go look in the room over the milk house."

The four mount the stairs and enter through the many-paned door. Side by side in the empty front room stand a bear and a barrel. The bear is dark brown, its four legs on wheels, and is big enough to ride. They all make a dash but Craig gets there first and straddles it. He promptly discovers a metal ring in the middle of the bear's shoulders. He pulls it and the bear says, in a low weary voice, "Uuunh." Craig scoots the bear forward. It turns out that one of the wheels is only half a wheel; the bear lists to the side and dunks when it rolls. But that hardly matters. It is a wonderful bear! They take turns riding it and making it go "Uuuunh."

They then turn their attention to the barrel. It is larger than the chocolate powder barrel in the old schoolhouse, larger than the copper sulphate barrel. It's open at the top but covered with tucked-in newspapers. They peel back the papers and make their flabbergasting find. *The barrel is filled with toys!*

After a stunned moment they reach in and start grabbing them out, loudly laying claim, until Joan declares that everything in the barrel has to belong to all of them, just like the bear has to, unless there's something nobody else wants. Patsy, Jackie and Craig can see the justice of this. They also agree when Joan suggests they remove things one at a time, and examine them together.

Where did all the toys come from? That's easy to figure out. The rich relatives have four daughters, long grown up. The Dougan kids have never known these second cousins, except that Joan once met the youngest, Betsy. Betsy was visiting at the farm and riding a horse, and she told Joan, who was trotting along behind her, breathless with admiration, to go away and quit bothering her — she was too little and might get hurt. Joan was outraged to be ordered off her own fields by a virtual stranger. Forever after she has resented Betsy Bosworth.

But now all is forgiven. Somebody put the Bosworth girls' outgrown toys in a barrel, and sent the barrel up to the farm along with the marble-top tables and bird's-eye maple.

The barrel is a cornucopia. Wonder after wonder pours from it. There is a rag doll as tall as Patsy, with a smiling face and yellow yarn braids and a real child's dress and pinafore. Elastic bands are sewed to the bottoms of her feet, so that you can put your feet through the straps and dance with her. There is a metal platter painted with houses and trees and streams and bridges and a train station. When you wind a key on the underside, a little train runs round and round a groove in the edge of the platter. Most of the other windup toys no longer work, but one that still does is an amazement:

a little tin woman, with long tin skirts and her hair in a mob cap. She holds a tin carpet sweeper with bristles that really go around, and wound up she darts here and there erratically pushing the sweeper stiffly before her. She has a no-nonsense expression. Her name is printed on her apron: Bizzy Lizzy.

There are alphabet blocks and anchor blocks. There are books, among them several fat volumes of *Chatterbox,* which turn out to be bound collections of old children's magazines with games and puzzles and continued mystery stories. These come from England, and Jackie immediately adores them. There are toys with missing parts, and parts with missing toys. There are games with no directions jostling for space with games complete in their boxes. There are three ornate cut-glass perfume bottles, elegantly stoppered, fit for a queen's dressing table. The bottles are empty but each retains a trace of faraway fragrance.

These, and some of the toys, come wrapped in funny papers. The four spread the papers out and see comics they recognize, but most are from before their time, such as Little Nemo and Krazy Kat.

When the call for noon dinner comes, they hurry back to the Little House, each carrying a choice item to show Mother and Daddy. Joan brings the beautiful perfume bottles, Patsy clasps Bizzy Lizzy, Jackie and Craig between them lug the bear.

Their parents are happy to share their delight. Mother makes one rule. The barrel toys are to be kept over the milk house, for the Little House is cluttered enough, and the long window box is already crammed to the top with toys. That is all right with the four.

Though usually worn and sometimes broken, the new toys are special for several reasons. Fundamentally, they have appeared out of nowhere, totally unsolicited, imagined, longed for, or deserved. It is not Christmas or Easter or anyone's birthday. They are pure manna from heaven. Then, because the Bosworth cousins are so much older, their toys are not the familiar ones in the stores and advertisements. Where could anyone possibly go to purchase a Bizzy Lizzy? Her day has come and gone. Add to that the wealth of the Bosworths. The toys they purchased are expensive ones, from unusual catalogues or Chicago department stores like Marshall Field's. They sit on a higher shelf in the economic toy shop than most of the Dougan kids' toys, however plentiful.

But all this is not enough to make the room over the milk house Paradise. There is a final factor. At the Little House, play goes on on the living room rug. Extensive villages outlined with blocks and peopled with small ceramic dolls and dogs, elaborate tinker toy or Lincoln log extravaganzas, can last only an afternoon. Sometimes Mother is persuaded to let a particularly absorbing creation stay up till the following day. Then everybody has to be careful to step over it or around it, including the family pets who are particularly obtuse about such matters.

But over the milk house, the spacious room is totally theirs. No grown-up presence taints it. Week after week, the four can play on the sunny floor and never have to pick up anything. *No one ever, ever, ever says: "Time to put your things away."* When they return, everything is as they left it.

But earthly paradises do not last. Patsy arrives at the room one day to find it bare. She is stricken, and so are Joan and Jackie and Craig. They rush to find out what has happened. Their parents don't know. But the answer is soon forthcoming. Grama has decided they've played with the toys long enough. It's time for Trever's children to have a turn. After all, they are Bosworth cousins too. So, like Moo Moo in the night, the barrel has vanished. It has been loaded up and shipped to Jerry and Karla.

Daddy says it's also history repeating itself in another way; his Grandmother Delcyetta swiped his toys when he didn't pick them up and hid them in her bottom drawer. They weren't found till she died.

It doesn't make them feel any better. "You at least got them *back*," Patsy wails. She never does get over losing Bizzy Lizzy.

But two things are saved from Armageddon. Jackie happens to have a volume of *Chatterbox* under her pillow at the Little House. And Craig has only recently dragged the bear that says "Uuunh" over to the playhouse, as a guest at a stuffed animal tea party.

Jacqueline Jackson

◆

The Great Hayloft in the Sky
(From *The Round Barn*)

Daddy has a health scare when he's fifty-seven or so. He goes breakfastless to the dentist; emerging from the office he lights a cigarette. He gets dizzy, blacks out and collapses in the hall. At the hospital he undergoes tests. His doctor tells him he's had a very small stroke; his arteries are vulnerable and he must never smoke another cigarette. Daddy quits smoking.

A new American Breeders Service vet, Les Larson, has been coming down to the farm about once a month to work with Daddy on infertility problems in the Dougan herd. Les has devised a little plywood shelf that he can move from windowsill to windowsill in the round barn as he works along behind the cows. It holds the paperwork on each animal.

Daddy leans on the little shelf, telling Les a story. A prop slips and the shelf tips. Daddy crashes to the floor. He's greatly relieved when he learns it wasn't dizziness that caused his tumble.

"I thought this was it," he confides to Les. "I thought I was looking over Jordan — but it was only the manure trough."

Later he expands to Mother on the Great-Hayloft-in-the-Sky. "I rather hope it's like that," he says. "I'd feel at home. The pearly gates will be stanchions — a little easier to squeeze through than a needle's eye, though I don't have to worry about being a rich man. Angels. They're obvious, with their big eyes and long lashes and soft breath and sweet voices continually mooing and hymning before the throne. But where is the throne? It'd have to be at the top of the silo, up there with the pigeons. The only thing I'd not care about would be swimming that river. Do you suppose it's narrow enough to step across?"

"Maybe you aren't destined for heaven," Mother says. "What do you see as the other place? A pigsty?"

Daddy is shocked. "Oh, no! There's a place for them there, too. One of the many mansions. Why, heaven might be all one big wallow. Maybe there's no space for us there, at all. I can't for the life of me see why God would want humans. Except Gramp, of course. What is God, anyway? The Great I-Am."

Mother quotes Popeye: "I yam what I yam."

"God as sweet potato," Daddy muses. "That opens a whole new realm. I wonder where among the Dominions and Powers the rutabegies rank?"

Many years later, Daddy comes back from being a pallbearer at a funeral. He's depressed by the whole event. At the table he announces gloomily, "When I die, just dig a posthole and drop me in."

"Head first or feet first?" a granddaughter asks.

"It depends what direction you think I'm going," Ron Dougan replies.

Jacqueline Jackson

◆

Poem

My cat died in the night,
curled up beside me as she often does.
I knew she had died even in my sleep
for in my sleep I am always conscious
of her moving, of her getting up to leave near dawn.
She lay relaxed; she had been frantic for a moment, last night,
wild-eyed, trying to scale the blanket and I'd had to help her
onto the bed. I had stroked her as we both settled down. Earlier,
she had purred twice. It was her twenty-first birthday;
she weighed less than three pounds.

My father died last week; he would have been ninety-four
next month. My last words to him on the day before he died were,
see you Thursday, and his last words were to my daughter —
my cat's owner since she was ten, twenty-one years ago — who
accompanied my father into surgery, asking him to try to be
comfortable on the gurney, and he responding, "That's easier to say
than do!" When she called me, she said, "Mom, he wasn't suffering,
and he wasn't afraid — not like last time." Last time, after she and I
and her oldest sister had saved him from cardiac arrest, we'd held
him down for four hours after the operation till it was safe to give
him a sedative; it took all our combined strength. Then, his eyes
had been like a wild animal's in a trap.

We gave Dad five more years of a good life.

I like to think my care gave Mighty Mouse, that feisty, loving cat
that ruled this house, five more years of her cat-life than she would
have had otherwise. I dug a hole just now on the spot by the tulips
where she lay in the sun, yesterday afternoon, and I laid her in,
still relaxed, with no shroud, only earth above and below.
I covered her with black prairie earth.

Dad, I kissed his swiftly cooling hands good-bye, after I pulled
the plug, because I couldn't kiss his face — it was so unDadlike,
swollen from the fluids his kidneys could not express. His body went
to ashes, and some of them flew in the wind over the edge of Beloit,
those that didn't make it into the posthole he'd asked to be buried in.
Some of them flew onto his children and grandchildren, but I was
not downwind. The video will tell us who was blessed with his dust.
Afterwards, we troweled in black dirt from the farm, Carrington
loam over gravel, the best farmland in the world, to fill his posthole.
I have not yet had time to grieve for my father, death keeps one
so busy — while life does not relax its demands to let you care for
the dead, to give you grieving time. Weddings have honeymoons;
why isn't there a grief moon for the living?

And how can I weep for my cat when I have not yet wept
for my father?

I am weeping for you both, Dad and Mighty Mouse, and for myself,
and for all those to whom I have given the awefull gift of life,
and those from whom I have taken this gift, and for all the hopes
and dreams that have been fulfilled, and for all the hopes
and dreams that haven't.

Deborah Brothers

◆

From *Sidewinder*

The old man could not bring himself to finish cutting the calloused skin off his heel once the girl stopped to talk. He had lived alone for close to seventy years, yet there are certain codes of behavior that one does not depart from, no matter how shut off one is from the world. At first, it was her greeting that made him pause just as the blade of his pearl-handled pocketknife had begun to penetrate the hard wrinkled rind. He tried to stop abruptly, but he did nothing abrupt anymore. The brain said, "stop," the signal traveled down the arm, to the hand and to the knife to stop, and yet the blade still trembled like the last leaf in winter.
"Hey, look at me!" she'd said, and he'd stopped cutting as best he could and looked up to see a girl of about ten or eleven at the edge of his lawn on a pair of orange painted stilts, her head a good three feet above his. The stilts took him by complete surprise.
The girl stood sideways to the tiny yard, bony feet securely planted on the footrests. She made sure that solid wood stood between her body and that of the man in the rusting lawn chair. She felt there was nothing to fear, but she had never spoken to him before, and there was that knife. Nothing wrong in being ready to leave.
She had encountered danger before and knew about making quick getaways. One time, a drunken man had tried to attack her on a small bridge at the park near her old house. She'd just gotten good enough on her stilts to walk the couple blocks without falling one time. Proudly, she'd climbed down to look for crawdad claws near the water. The man flew over the bridge in a red pick-up then skidded to a halt. Yelling and swearing, he hurtled out of his truck toward her, swinging a tire jack like a mace over his head.

She only hesitated a second before she jumped on the stilts and clomped by him. That's when she found out she could run on her stilts for several blocks — in fact, becoming famous in her old neighborhood for her stilt-walking abilities — but it was her only athletic triumph; she was uncoordinated otherwise, the long legs skinny twins to the orange poles that supported them several hours every day.

She spoke to the old man again. "My sister ran away last night but my mom found her at some girl's house." Her short blonde hair was frizzy and coarse. It bushed out crookedly as though a small wild animal hunkered down on her head. "She told Mom that this girl was a good friend, but we'd never heard of her before — did you ever run away?"

The old man looked her in the face. Bangs nearly covered her large brown eyes. But he could see into them. Strange eyes. Brown shot through with specks of orange. She stood in place on the stilts, but somehow the man sensed movement and something else that made him feel uncomfortable. "That your mom calling you?" he grunted suddenly, nodding toward the next block.

Another child might have spun around on the stilts in an about-face on the sidewalk and departed. The girl stayed. "No. Mom's not home now." She tossed her head and looked behind the man, as if she really just stopped to admire the way the honeysuckle grew up the side of his small brown house.

"Well. Guess I'll say good-bye," he said.

"Are you going somewhere?"

"Aren't you?" he asked, and gripped the metal arm of the chair.

"Do you know why I came over here?" she said suddenly, pushing back the fluff of bangs with her elbow. He shut his eyes, unable to look at her as she spoke. "I thought that a witch lived here, but it's just you. Do you believe me?"

"What is there to believe or not believe?" He kept his eyes closed.

"What's your name?" She looked at him and waited, staring hard. He could see a bit of his reflection in the depths of her eyes: his raised eyebrows, his wrinkled forehead.

"Ikey." It sounded like a cough. If the girl dared laugh or asked him to repeat the name, he didn't know what he would do. But she didn't.

"What's your last name?" she asked instead.

"Just Ikey." It was as if a weight were off of him. His hands felt steady, his heart beat in the right rhythm again. But he wanted to go inside.

She waited for Ikey to ask for her name. Instead, he smoothly cleaned both sides of his pocketknife on the thigh of his brown pants, pushed the blade in, and slid his feet into house shoes.

"Good day to you." He stiffly arose, grabbing the chair to steady himself. A leaf had attached itself to the bottom of the left shoe, but Ikey did not notice, or did not take the time to remove it.

"My name's Kay!" she yelled. He continued to walk, hunched over, toward the house. "Did you hear me, Ikey? I'll come back over later, okay?" The man paused at the door. Kay saw the oblique glance and it was enough for her. "Don't you worry. I'll be back soon." She spun around and began to run on the stilts.

The "clump, clump, clump" of wood meeting concrete echoed like the toll of a dull bell. When Ikey was sure Kay was not looking in his direction, he nodded his head, biting his top lip. "Yes, you'll be back."

Deborah Brothers

◆

Leather Peace Ring

When I was ten years old and in the fifth grade my best friend gave me a present: a sterling St. Christopher's medal on a silver chain. "He's supposed to protect you when you travel," Carl said. He may have sensed I was going to need this protection. I didn't sense it then, but I was glad to receive the gift.

A couple of weeks later I was wearing the medal when we had a wreck. Mom and Dad had argued again and Mom decided we would stay at her parents' house for a night or two. My sister, Robyn, was sixteen and could have driven, but as it was raining hard Mom wouldn't let her. Mark and I tried to keep our distance from each other, so he was in the backseat while I camped out with pillows and *Eight Cousins* in the tail of our white and wood station wagon. Just about ten miles outside of town, the wipers stopped working.

"Damn," Mom said, pulling into the parking lot of a small cafe at Crab Orchard. She and Mark got out, popped the hood, and tried to see if there were broken wires. No luck. Someone inside the restaurant suggested the mechanic's garage about a mile up the road.

Robyn and Mark were both employed as lookouts, one for each side of the car, and even though they rolled their windows down all the way, sticking their heads out into the storm, neither could really see much. No one saw the car Mom drove into as she pulled out of the parking lot. Luckily, no one got hurt. The livid driver of the other vehicle screamed at Mom that he'd only just gotten his car back from the repair shop due to an accident caused by another *damn* woman.

Within an hour, insurance information had been exchanged and the wipers fixed at Bud's Garage up the road. "Bud" shared the same nickname as my father. "Of course," my mom commented with a smirk. Everything even vaguely connected with Dad brought out that look in my mom.

"Good thing I was wearing this," I said, pointing to the St. Christopher's medal. Then they all got the smirk. About the only thing I knew about religion was that my sister and I, who shared a bed, raced each other to say our prayers at night. Mine, if slowed down, could have been understood as the standard "Now I Lay Me Down" with "God Bless Mommy, Daddy, Robyn, Mark/ Everybody else in heaven/ Everybody else in the world/ Amen" tacked on the end. Of course, I never slowed it down. Although I still couldn't comprehend how the metal man worked his protective rituals, I was just glad my friend Carl knew the ways of the saints.

As 1969 wore on and it was clear that Mom and Dad were divorcing, I wondered if St. Chris needed some help. For a few days I didn't eat lunch with my daily 35 cents, instead using the money for better magic — a leather band with an attached metal peace symbol on top. Because of the Vietnam War, peace signs were all the rage, and the symbol seemed to suggest something to me. Something stronger even than a religious icon. I rode my bike to the Ben Franklin at Parker Plaza to buy the ring. I was wearing it the day we left our house with Mom and moved into a dive with slanting wooden floors and a spooky dirt basement.

The day we moved our belongings from O'Gara Street, I jumped out of the station wagon — right as Mom was pulling away. My left foot made shaky contact, and I sprawled over the concrete curb, ran through the yard, and burst inside our old house carrying my book. Dad sat in the bare front room on an upright box. He was sobbing into his hands. "Here, Daddy," I said, handing over *Trixie Beldon*. "Maybe this will help." I ran back to the car petting my ring, sliding my finger over the smooth metal like a nun with rosary beads.

Walking to school from the new neighborhood was strange, and I couldn't seem to synchronize my walk-time with Carl's. We had been put into different rooms that year, too, and I hardly saw him anymore.

There was one girl at school who had picked on me for a couple of years. Her name was Tamara. She and her friends liked to bug me about my clothes, my glasses, my perpetual books — the usual. But what happened wasn't usual. I'd had enough one day and screamed, "I hope you die!" right up in her face. She and her entourage merely giggled.

A week later while en route to St. Louis for a Christmas shopping trip, Tamara was killed when she was thrown out the window of a travel bus as it skidded and crashed on a slippery bridge. My mother was cutting my bangs when we heard the news. It was a Saturday evening and because it was the season, *The Littlest Angel* was on television, and I was watching it as Mom trimmed. Robyn ran through the front door, bringing in cold air and news about the accident. I began retching into the newspaper I held in my lap to catch the hair. I vomited the rest of the night.

After the funeral, Tamara's friend, Rebecca, shouted at me in front of the rest of our class, "You're a witch, you killed her!" A few days later, my mom remarried and we moved again. This time I changed schools, where no one would know I was really a witch.

Within another six months, my father remarried and my sister was getting married, too. She was going to have a baby. Robyn moved out of our bed and into her husband's, forty miles away. My nightly prayers had to change, and there was no longer any need to race through them. In fact, there wasn't much of a reason to even say them. I still had my ring, though. Or maybe it had me.

Robyn and Jim planned to take me to a fancy restaurant one night. Mom had made me a green and blue flowered "maxi" dress. I put it on and waited by the door. Robyn glanced at my hand. There was a problem.

"That jewelry is awful looking. Don't you want to look pretty?" my sister asked.

"I won't take it off."

"Take off the ring and I'll loan you some jewelry to wear tonight."

"This is pretty." I knew that was a lie. I'd been wearing the ring every day for over a year then. The smooth, tan leather was roughened up and had darkened.

My young brother-in-law, whom I adored, walked into the room and Robyn got him to her side immediately. Jim asked me to consider going without jewelry, or switching to Robyn's. I wouldn't listen to either of them. I wouldn't back down. But I did get to eat leftover lobster tail — brought back to me in a small, brown paper bag — and only got a bit of grease on my ring.

During P.E. class in the seventh grade, the peace ring caught on my gym clothes basket. The leather, already blackened and turned-up on the edges, split completely apart, and the ring fell to the floor.

I panicked. "Anybody got a safety pin?"

Debbie Boots did, and I used it to fasten the ring together, sighing with relief as I slipped it back on my finger.

As junior high progressed, the ring morphed into compost from constant contact with bathing and sweat. My mom noticed. "When are you going to take that damn thing off?" she asked. I had no answer for her. The ring was with me through fights with my stepfather, my brother's night in jail, and the birth of my father's new daughter. I clasped its broken pieces to my finger as I prayed on it at night.

Finally, the day came where Mother couldn't stand my ring anymore. The leather looked, well . . . no other word for it, rotten. The metal symbol was black and green now instead of silver. Even the safety pin holding the ring together had tarnished and buckled. "Take it off, Debby," Mother said. "Throw it away." I held my finger near my nose and sniffed. It stank.

It was the summer of 1973 when I appeared at the supper table with my finger ringless. After all, I would start high school in a couple of months, and I certainly didn't need to pretend that a ring gave me protection. My mom noticed and commented, "Good girl," and I gave her a small smile.

That night, as I stripped off my clothes and got ready for bed, I draped my bra over my chest of drawers, carefully peeled the peace ring from my chest, and then tucked the jewelry inside the dangling bra cup. I held my nightshirt away from my body and glanced down at my right breast with its embossed peace sign indentation. I would see that mark every night for another year at least. It was enough to keep me safely as I slept.

Pat Martin

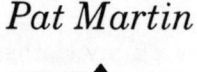

Poems

**1948: Taylorville, Illinois
Harry Truman's Whistle-Stop Campaign**

"It's cold," you said as a blizzard of orange
and yellow leaves rushed past the window.
"Better wear your snowsuit and mittens, Annie."

You bundled me up like when we went Halloweening.
I asked where my treat sack was and you just laughed —
        You just laughed.

At the sound of the train whistle
you pushed me out the door.
"Better get a move on!
We don't want to miss the President!"

You pulled me
    a fuzzy penguin
        so fast down the street
            my feet

        barely touched the sidewalk:

Your own coat unbuttoned
your own hair flying in the wind.

Grandma's Story: "I Never Knew"

I never knew if Mama hated Daddy because he drank
or if he drank because she hated him.
But I'd be so scared
when he'd stagger through the door
eyes like burned-out cinders
holding my face in his burly hands
planting wet kisses all around my writhing lips
at last he'd turn away disgusted
and then I'd creep into Mama's wardrobe
grab the knob on the back of the door handle
yank it as hard as I could
so the door would stay shut
reach up the sleeve of Mama's coat
pull down her soft wool scarf
scrunch it up and press it
tight over my ears
but I still heard snarls and growls
and ripping, falling brush
when a heavy body slammed against
the door of my hiding place
I held my breath
pulled my knees closer to my pounding heart
and then the darkness whispered another door
velvet soft
womb safe
rocking slowly back and forth
back and forth
and then a long sigh
caught in one of Daddy's traps
thrashed and moaned through the bed springs
after awhile the front door slammed
followed by Mama's heavy footsteps
heading toward the kitchen
as soon as my legs stopped cramping
I'd limp after her
and there she'd be hanging over the sink
her eyes covered by a wet dishrag
I'd ask, "Are you okay, Mama?"
And she'd answer through swollen lips,
"I'm fine, Eva May. Go on out and play now.
Supper'll be ready in a bit."

Taproot

The mourning star glitters remote
against the mauve sky visible
through the kitchen window
above Daddy's hollow chair
as I sip my lukewarm coffee
the sky turns luminous
and the clouds float like lazy pink salamanders
now a nomad breeze disturbs the golden dream
of the few remaining Sweet Gum leaves
not so long ago this same Sweet Gum
was a sapling Daddy and I dug up
in Danziger's woods down the road
careful not to injure its taproot
we carried it home proudly upright
I held it outside this very window
while Daddy dug a hole just the right size
to hold the taproot and its willowy shoot
and then he let me pat the dirt
around its trunk "Firmly,"
he said, "so it will stand
through the night"
bewitched I danced round and round the tree
and didn't even want to go in for supper
first thing in the morning I ran downstairs
barefoot across the wet grass
to where the sapling still stood
and hugged it to make sure
it was still alive
yesterday it took six men
to carry Daddy so quiet
to a hole someone else had dug
just the right size for him
as his casket was lowered
Mother and I shivered and waited
until it was time
to lift a shovelful of dirt
and drop it into his hibernation chamber
seeming to reach as deep
into the worm-eaten shadows
as the full grown Sweet Gum's taproot
only this time there was no dancing
and the dirt will have to settle by itself.

The Little Red Car

Impatient to be on your way
you barely had time for one more hug
before you dashed through the rainswept
air and jumped into your little red car
packed with law books
new suits
fuzzy pink bathroom towels
bedding
and wild dreams.

Leaning against the porch railing
I waited while you turned on
the windshield wipers
adjusted the rear-view mirror
backed onto the street
paused for a moment
a drawn arrow homing in on its bull's-eye
you shifted into drive
and jerked forward on your way
to the skyscrapers of Chicago.

I watched you all the way down England Street
and still watched for a glimpse
of your little red car
in the gaps between houses
as you drove north on Houston.

Spilling back through many soft rains
I slip into small pink ballerina slippers
a bubblegum bank
the big yellow Pac Man Mike won for you
at the State Fair
seam-split khaki walking shorts
stumble under one hammering protest
and you are gone for sure.

Strangely Comforted

In the primal morning light
a sparrow huddled on the wet
grass at the base of the birdbath
its left wing nearly useless
flopped it lopsided midway
to the back door where it rested
hunched and broken
with its head curled
on the crooked wing
darkness stalked its lidless eyes
Max lunged at the bird
but I jerked his leash
dragged him on and firmly attached
his collar to the chain that held him
on the way back I stopped perplexed
beside the exhausted bird
"What can I do? What can I do?"
"Don't touch! Don't touch!"
came the whispered reply
softly another sparrow
bright brown flecks on a plump gray body
landed next to the wounded bird
nudged its shoulder with its beak
lingered an instant and then flew away
by the time I brought Max back in
the sparrow lay motionless already blending
with the earth that held it
strangely comforted I closed the door
and left for work.

Ambushed

damp air charged with the essence
of pork sizzling on a charcoal grill
filters through my third-floor window
draws me away from the manuscript
I've been studying
ambushed by muted chatter
soft laughing
the promise of music
I gaze upon a jazz ensemble
gathered on the red cobblestones below
my watch says half an hour to lunchtime
back to the document
each line billows
unfocused eyes stray
toes and fingers captured
a rogue spirit infiltrates the window
sprinkles shimmering
and then scatters as the elevator bell
quick as a silver dream
blazes along its dark shaft
a nimble outlaw lifts my purse
and blinks me through the sudden door.

Warm Satin Milk

Absorbed in a hollow wreath of love
I bide pianissimo
hoping for release
from my shame-filled purgatory
the plum-colored mouth
that opens into a rigid vessel
cut persistently
until the walls disintegrate
in a smeared humiliation
a procession of broken arches
christening slippers impregnated
with a bottomless stench
that rises through
swaddling clothes
crying for Mother's ripe nipples
to fill the empty gorge
and mend the brokenness
with her warm satin milk.

I Don't Belong

I don't belong in this perforated body
heart pounding against my mutilated ribs
clinging to life like an infant
who won't let go her mother's nipple
tubes up my nose
needles in my arm
drainage pumping out
one with the purring technology
that keeps me here
so dependent on a source
that can be taken away instantly
when Mother's breast erupts
hurls fire and ashes and mutant cells
high into the sky
no nurturing teat this inflamed summit
no warm flesh to cuddle up to
just a furnace where the mythic flames of hell
flicker like the tongue of a prehistoric gila monster
nabbing endless prey
I close my eyes
build a fire wall myself inside
huddle close to the earth
beneath the smoke and flames and ash
but there's no protection against hot lava
raw fire melts the rocks
rolls down the mountain
into all the valleys
death croons along the molten fissures
no escape can't run that fast
what isn't burned away or melted
is embalmed beneath a suffocating blanket.

Trailing Enough Remembering

The weather-beaten year collapses
in a blue-dark mirror
drowsy earth jolted
by quicksilver rain
and a protestant gale
hurls a crippling rebuke
at a pale small bloom
that resisted autumn's
yawning undertow
craving after a field
of pungent
magenta
bellydancers
Cyclopean mutiny
the consort's dreaming rainbow
reflects a frostbitten fusion
the flowers that yielded
at last
beneath the wild sun
trailing enough remembering
the pythoness' gentle halo straddles the echo
of fields in ruin
and the moon sweats love.

The Prophet's Touch

The prophet's touch warms
winter's parched bones
sings green-eyed Spring
into my snowdreams
calls back the redwing blackbirds
stirs the nest-building instinct
robinsong on the widening breeze
lifts crocuses, daffodils, tulips,
bends beside the awakened pond
inspires spears of asparagus
backtracks to the roots
of the redbud and hackberry trees
opens the way for iris and peonies
to push through earth's willing crust
tomato plants preparing to fill roomy plots
bow gallant before onions and radishes and lettuce
and I sit at the picnic table
notebook and pen in front of me
try to capture the essence
preserve it like blackberry jam
but the afternoon sun
passes over our honeyed euphoria
slashing the brief day
the prophet becomes a cook
swiftly chops round steak
slices green peppers
pours stewed tomatoes
sprinkles mozzarella
and lets the whole concoction simmer.

Carol Manley

◆

Gramma and the Butcher

Gramma had battles with the butcher. She was a small round childlike person whose soft little body was drawn by gravity into layers like the down swept branches of a Christmas tree. In her platform rocker, doodling on her Puffs tissue box and watching *As the World Turns,* Gramma appeared to be perfectly harmless. From time to time, though, the embers that smoldered deep within her would blaze up during the closing credits of *Search for Tomorrow* and she would march off purposefully to the Piggly-Wiggly, with fire in her eye, in search of the perfect cut of meat.

Gramma knew groceries. Her family outhouse had been decorated with cardboard posters of Kellogg's Cornflakes from the store her father once owned. She had adored her father. She said he looked just like Gregory Peck, and his good looks had cursed her childhood. Female teachers had watched her relentlessly, breathless for her to commit the most minor transgressions so that they might demand conferences with this handsome man.

Gramma always had carefully contrived shopping lists. No one ever saw her buy basic food. Sugar and flour must have gotten into her kitchen through some secret plotting of their own because the magic list included only the most recently patented miracles — no-bake cheesecake and instant mashed potatoes.

Gramma also invested heavily in grocery items that offered special inducements. It was Blue Bonnet Margarine, or maybe Imperial, that became a big part of our lives by promoting costume jewelry. Gramma saved up box tops and box bottoms and order entry forms. In return, the mailman showered her with packages — strings of fake pearls and gold ballerina pins, soup mugs and cereal spoons. One year we ate enough cornflakes for Gramma to order four Linda Lou dolls, each with a carrying case and four complete outfits.

Meat, though, was its own reward. There were no outside inducements to tempt a woman into buying meat. The drama with beef was entirely in the hunt.

Divine inspiration for Gramma's grocery safaris could strike at any time, but never on a Friday. Friday was the traditional day for suspenseful endings on her soap operas. Cliff-hangers usually involved ominous strangers arriving to reveal the secret of someone's past or sudden dramatic illnesses where babies needed organ transplants which required revelations about the child's real father.

Gramma religiously followed *As the World Turns* and never scheduled another event on Fridays when the action was sure to get tense. She watched the show every day with a cup of tea and a couple of Lorna Doones or Vienna Fingers. The tea cooled and left rings in the cup while Gramma balanced her attention between the television screen and her crossword puzzle book. With Grampa's old reading glasses halfway down her nose, and a Puffs tissue box turned upside down for a flat writing surface, Gramma would ink in the across and down columns of the crossword.

When the inspiration to shop struck Gramma, she would set the Puffs tissue box aside, hang her apron on the back of her bedroom door and shake out a touch of talcum powder. She would run a comb through her wispy, gray hair and roll each of a pair of seamed stockings up to her knees. She would change from one faded print cotton dress to an identical one, powder her face and go. The trip to Piggly-Wiggly was accomplished solely on the strength of her two stout legs. Gramma never drove a car.

On Saturdays, my mother and grandmother would apply smears of rich, red lipstick and my dad would drive them to Rockford. Lipstick was not required, though, for attendance at the local Piggly-Wiggly. When the primping was done, Gramma was cased in invisible armor. She became a woman warrior. Wheeling her little wire grocery cart along behind her, Gramma's little round body propelled her down Menominee Street, prepared to do battle.

Piggly-Wiggly was about six blocks from home at what had once been the edge of town. By that time, both Dad and Grampa were firmly planted in the little cemetery behind the store. They rested in the shade of a crumbling little building, built by Frank Lloyd Wright under an assumed name while he was under contract to Louis Sullivan. The cemetery was barely visible from the Piggly-Wiggly parking lot. Ace Hardware and Walgreen Drug stores had been built alongside the grocery, completing a strip mall fortress between the living and the dead.

Gramma looked neither right nor left on her march to Piggly-Wiggly. She kept her eyes straight ahead, her mind on her mission. I followed at a respectful distance, since I couldn't keep up. I was taller than Gramma and had the advantage of youth, but Gramma had the advantage of Purpose.

Piggly-Wiggly had rubber mats to activate the doors whenever you stepped on them. No other electronic devices warned of her approach, but the butcher on duty immediately smelled danger. Drying his hands on his stained, white apron, he emerged from the cutting room and stood stiffly behind the meat case. He would not look at Gramma. She would not look at him. But they were connected by a laser beam of electric tension. As Gramma approached, the man's muscles tightened visibly. He continued to look straight ahead. The other customers scattered. Gramma stepped up fearlessly, impervious to his powers of intimidation. One by one, she picked up each cellophane wrapped package of meat and examined it with her x-ray meat-buying vision. One had too much fat. One had too much bone. One looked too tough. Another was overpriced. As she rejected each piece of meat, Gramma, confident that no other customer would sink so low as to buy it either, flung each unacceptable package to the end of the meat case with all the force her seventy-year-old forearms could muster.

The butcher fumed. He grunted. He stepped forward, dramatically straightening the rows of bloody cuts while Gramma continued the desecration. She sniffed in indignation that anyone should offer such shoddy merchandise to be inspected by her expert eye. The butcher visibly restrained himself from picking up the old woman and ejecting her bodily from the store. Mortified, I slunk off to the magazine racks at the front of the store.

Free from association with my marauding grandmother at the back of the store, I compared publications. I was absorbed by the agony of indecision over which actor or rock star would be best for me to marry. I carefully considered my options, ultimately choosing my future mate from among those with the nicest hair. Arriving at a reasonable decision, and fortified for several days of romantic fantasy, I wistfully replaced the well-thumbed volumes in the magazine rack. My mother wouldn't allow this literature in the house.

With my romantic future fully resolved, I returned to the back of the store to check on Gramma. I lurked between the cereal and baking supplies, waiting for her to conclude her assault. Packages of meat lay like discarded clothing, scattered across the meat case where Gramma had flung them. Her search for the perfect cut of meat was unrelenting. Where his original hairline might have been, the butcher had beads of sweat, prominent as jewels. His apron was rumpled and his spine was no longer erect. He was a beaten man. With a sigh of resignation, he disappeared back into the meat cutting room and emerged with one singular packet of meat in his hand. Pretending to ignore Gramma, the butcher set down the roast and poked it with one finger in Gramma's direction. She picked it up and raised it to the light. "Well," she said cautiously after scrutinizing it from every angle, "I guess this one will have to do."

The butcher crumpled against the wall for a minute in exhaustion before heading to the back room for a cigarette. I reflected on the scene. The movie magazines which colored my imagination had planted a question in my mind. Could this little carnivorous drama possibly be one of those inexplicable manifestations of sexual tension between a man and a woman? I looked at Gramma, still glowing slightly from her triumph. She smiled, still looking frowsy in her cotton dress. I looked at her for an answer. "I think I did pretty well," she said.

Carol Manley

◆

Nine and a Half Months

By my calculations I was nine and a half months pregnant, living on the fifth floor of a building where the only thing scarier than the elevator was the other tenants. It was probably just a little prenatal paranoia that made me cautious of other residents. They were all too busy drinking, fighting among themselves, dodging the landlord, yelling at their children, or talking back to the voices in their heads to be a threat to me.

The elevator shouldn't have been too frightening either, since it would have had to be running before it could actually malfunction. Because it was chronically shut down for some mysterious and imperceptible repairs, there was little chance of anybody ever being in it if the cable chose to snap or the electrical circuits decided to burst. The wrought iron accordion gates of it were quite lovely when they were not completely obscured by signs from the landlord disclaiming any responsibility for the multiple injuries you would surely sustain if you ever got in the thing.

The bed I owned was only slightly more inviting than the elevator. It projected out of a balding green sofa and would have been called a hideabed if the frame hadn't gotten bent and ended the bed's hiding days forever. The frame was quite solid around the edges, with metal tubing defining a route that connected the three legs that were even with a fourth leg that was not. The center of the bed wasn't so well supported. The thin mattress was suspended on a curious network of springs and wires, some connecting each other and some connecting to nothing but the snagged mattress cover from which the not-to-be-removed tag was ominously missing.

This invention was several inches less than knee high, which presented a dilemma. Once lowered onto the surface, my most pregnant parts were incapable of rising again without exhaustive effort and planning. With my increasing inability to get out of bed came a growing pressure on my bladder. The amount of time necessary to maneuver myself out of bed came closer and closer to completely filling the intervals between trips to the bathroom until most of my day was spent wistfully watching the bed rock on its uneven legs while I wondered whether I could possibly get myself into it and back out before I had to pee again.

Options for other activities were severely limited. It was mid-July of an exceptionally hot summer. My amniotic bulge, so happily simmering away, seemed to throw off steam, keeping me covered in a constant coat of pregnant perspiration. I completely abandoned any effort to get dressed, and my unwillingness to wear clothes consequently limited the number of places I was welcome and activities in which I was able to participate.

I lay around the apartment, one smoldering bulge of pink and white flesh with disproportionately stubby arms and legs projected uncomfortably out to the sides. One day, with my eyes roaming listlessly over this great hump, it came into my mind exactly how much I had come to resemble a beached whale. This revelation I immediately interpreted as a personal message from God. I knew then that I must name this child Jonah or risk the wrath of an irate deity. In those brief, heretical moments when I considered other names, I cringed inwardly and watched through my unwashed windows for the bolts of lightning that were sure to strike.

The petty annoyances of pregnancy were compounded by the fact that I'd been pregnant for twenty-seven and a half of the previous thirty-three months. I was beginning to suspect that in one spectacular act of conception I had been inseminated for life and I feared that I would be pregnant forever.

The perpetrator of these pregnancies had developed his own third trimester strategy. As the time of birth came close, he fled the state. He carried with him the fruits of my two previous summers. The older of the pair was not yet two years old and had been enormously helpful to me, retrieving like a terrier anything I dropped on the floor. Since her first few faltering steps, I'd been relieved of the responsibility of bending over, and I missed her more and more each day as unreachable clutter accumulated around my ankles.

The nutritional sins of my first two trimesters began to haunt me, and, in a single, impulsive attempt at redemption, I spent every cent I had on spinach, liver and tomatoes, the holy trinity of food groups that would surely compensate for everything else if only I could somehow pass them on to this slumbering child without having to eat them.

There is a theory that pregnant women crave the foods that are most necessary for the baby's development. If that was true, my baby was in desperate need of chocolate milk and taco chips after I had recklessly squandered the grocery money on spinach.

I waddled through the apartment without a cent of cash or a stitch of clothes. Pacing from the table with that god-awful healthy food to the bed with its deceptive promise of comfort, I began to fear that I had fallen into a void of time and space. I watched the clock, hoping to catch it in the act of slipping extra minutes into each hour of these endless days. Unable to concentrate on anything else for more than a few minutes at a time, I carefully studied the great bulge in front of me. It was no crystal ball.

At night the moonlight filtered in through the lace curtains, throwing delicate patterns onto the bed while I lay awake pondering the mystery of it. It revealed nothing to me. Anytime I ventured onto the streets, toothless old women would emerge from the shadows, as if they were in some secret pact with my belly. They patted it without permission, and without exception announced that it was a boy.

Whatever it was, it was deeply content, satisfied to lie motionless for hours at a time. It shifted slightly from time to time, but never committed violence on me in the way that my two girls had, beginning their battles for freedom early, while I was too dazzled by them to protest. This one could not be riled to anger, even under the constant threat of spinach and liver.

So I spent my days, musing and napping, enjoying brief periods of peace until that pressure built up in my bladder. Then I would thrash around on my back like a capsized turtle until I could work up the momentum to hurl myself up and out of bed. At night I would drift to sleep, gazing out the window at the moon, round and white and so much smaller than my belly.

One night I woke up with a start, completely mortified to feel the puddle forming under my hips. Without pain or contractions, I didn't realize for several minutes that I was finally, mercifully, in labor.

I had experienced labor in hospitals before. I didn't like it. Throughout this pregnancy I'd secretly nursed the intention of having this baby at home, under the porch if necessary, like a cat. Cultural conditioning beat out instinct, though. I prepared to surrender myself to the authorities.

I had no phone in my apartment. I headed out into the night. Signs posted by the elevator reminded me that souls braver than myself had tried and failed to pilot that vehicle to safety. I waddled down the four flights of stairs and navigated the long dark hallway to the manager's apartment at the back of the building. There was no response, even as my knocking grew louder. Frustrated, I allowed my tired knuckles to come to rest on a sticker pasted to the door. I read the message. It said that the manager was armed and willing to shoot intruders. I decided to walk.

I stepped out into the moonlight. Wilson Avenue is not a street where women walk alone at night unless they are entrepreneurs of a certain sort, seeking to do business. I rested my hands on my belly, attempting to convey to the men cruising by in cars that I was otherwise occupied. I was determined to make it safely to the end of the block where lights flashed off and on at the all-night pizzeria.

Finally, without incident, I arrived at the pizzeria and patiently waited my turn in line. The man ahead of me wanted pepperoni and olives. I wanted a paramedic. Fortunately the chef on hand spoke enough English to grasp my condition. The ambulance arrived shortly. When it pulled up to the curb, I headed for the door. Out of the corner of my eye I saw one man turn to another. His words followed me out into the night.

"I told you she didn't want no pizza," he said.

Nancy Pistorius

◆

Poems

Reminders

sometimes i am standing
at the kitchen sink
peeling potatoes
or rinsing dishes
or staring into space
and then comes
the whispery surprise
    of your touch

the moment is transformed
i become new

and other times i am sitting
comfortably on the couch
reading a novel
or watching TV
or staring into space
and then comes
the sharp nudge
    of your indignation

i learn
you are also
your father's child

quickenings

i feel your first
faint stirrings tonight
a dream struggling
to awaken
soft and tentative
the patter of rain
on a thatched roof

muffled little mouse rustlings
deep within my womb
just to let me know

(oh so shyly)

that you are here

o butterfly fluttering
within your bright chrysalis
you nurture
my richest fantasies

i lie in the dark

trying to learn

your whispery touch

a voice

like the wings of an angel

my sweet secret child
gently you nudge
my innermost senses

o child of my body
you speak to me
from my very soul

waiting room

my body
no longer mine
but ours

each day you occupy
a bigger space
of my body

    my mind

    my thoughts

you even invade my dreams
you with the awesome power
of total helplessness

i think of you
when i eat
sleep
make love

nothing is secret
nothing is sacred

you are always there
nuzzling my ribs
as a gentle reminder

together
    we wait

now i see babies everywhere
    in grocery stores
        at county fairs
clinging to their mothers

you cling to me
with surprising fierceness
tiny fingers curled
upon the fabric of my dreams

now i can hear
you call me

my arms ache
to embrace you
my fingers long
to stroke your skin

o child of mine
sight unseen
let me learn you

to my husband, sleeping, in winter

your grey face mask on the pillow hardens
while clay from mine runs in chartreuse rivulets
a thousand wrinkles on the bedsheets divide us
your breath on my face smells like a foreign land

i scribble poems at midnight while you dream equations
my own dreams get tangled in your thick snarls of hair
yet your gentle snoring makes a familiar soothing music
your solid roots snake over me, a green entwining fortress

the cold kansas wind howls round our marriage bed

we are two wax candles waning in the night
yet on the ceiling overhead our shadows dance in circles
remembering smooth white beaches and soaring seagulls' cries

who gets the chicken heart?

my mother's job was to remember
whose turn it was each week

her hands deep in flour

she'd ponder

her forehead furrowed in little crosses

her mouth drawn tight as the skin on a persimmon

there was only one heart
there were two little girls
both of them solemnly waiting

sometimes my mother

could not remember

she always looked so tired
no matter which child she chose,
there'd be plenty of crying

it seemed to me
that she was always
on my sister's side

my mother only fried chicken
on saturdays
and sometimes my sister
would get the heart
three weeks in a row

it was so unfair

a chicken has just one heart
now i have just one child
but i never fry chicken
she's a vegetarian

birthday blues

one more birthday
and the tower of midnight
looms ahead
with far-reaching tentacles

i shrink back
into my smallest self
yet cannot escape
its beckoning shadow

the years wind across
my neck like ribbons
tightening
till my eyes bulge out

my palm's lifeline snakes
precariously along
then takes a jog and
falters

fire from wax candles
consumes my throat
i feel it searing
the slippery blood pulse

dry fear kindles the
leaping blue flames
i know not whose feet
tramp across my tombstone

no shooting stars
to guide futile wishes
the faces in my nightmares
are no longer strangers

obstinately i cling
to thin strands of seaweed
yet the current pulls
so rough
and hard

single exposure

i came to you
    utterly naked
crept before you
    without guile
cradled my soul in my
    trembling hands
so trustingly

you came
    with only your
        body
          bared

Sorry, Emily

Joy
is not
a thing with feathers

it mostly
runs around naked
as a new moon

Sue Daugherty

◆

Poems

For a daughter, nearly grown

I want you to birth yourself.

    I tell you
    you are beautiful
    and you say
    I know *you* think so.
    I tell you
    you are worthy of great respect
    and you say
    of course, *you* would think so.
    I say, shout, show endlessly
         I love you
    and you say
    you have to —
         you are my mother.

So I say now, *be* your mother.
Be your own mother.

Take care of yourself
as if someone inside you
needs you.
Protect her
before you even know her.

Love her
while you wait to discover if she will be lovable.
> When she sends you to your knees
> hot green over cold white
> muddying the clear water;
> When her becoming
> is unbecoming to you
>> distorts your image
>> disjoints your motion
>> disfigures your present —

    Love her.
Envision her while you wait.
Whisper to her when the wait is lonely,
    i want you
Near the end,
when time sleeps and you cannot
the awesome elasticity of tension
will stretch the doubting whisper to a certainty:
    I Want You.
Your labor this time
    a many-mothered mantra
    this is the path
    this is the path
    this is the path
It opens and the place arrives
look with my eyes
into your eyes
see written there:

    This I created

    and it is good.

Did he hurt you?

The first time
I heard that question
fall out of my mouth
she was freshly five
small but sturdy
her skin sun-browned
beneath its sandy dust coating
her doe eyes furtive
behind the sheer, ineffective curtain
of little girl hair.

I was proud of my control
pouring support and concern freely
for her to bathe in
while the heavy sediment of rage
floated down
settling
on the dark bottom
of my mother heart.

I was, perhaps,
less careful of that residue
the next time,
when she was ten,
her hair bobbed
too short for curtaining
eyes too often tear filled
in that year of divorce
and change and fear.
She ran to me then
no shy hiding
no fear of guilt
just terror
born as surely
of denied access to me
as of demanded access
to what was also hers alone.

Darkness darkened
bottom bowed
as the flakes which did not
splash out
with that question
floated down
mingled with vintage rage
and settled
on the dark bottom
of my heavy mother heart.

Five years passed, again.
Again, I asked the question.
Slowly, this time
it had to simmer
shake itself loose
separate itself
from its sedimented history
in order to rise
black and bitter
onto a tongue forewarned
the luminescent answer
already settled
on the dark bottom
of my heavy mother heart.

Did he hurt you?

A Requiem for Red

She sees something
I cannot see
when she gazes
lovingly
into his feral eyes
of blue or green or gray or brown
A subtle hunger, perhaps
behind or beneath
his ferocious appetite,
and it touches her.

Like one who's seen
the witch's candy cottage
or met fairies in the glen
debate
regarding the reality
of the seldom seen
is futile.
She has seen it
with her own eyes.

Enchanted
she draws near
feels his silvery silken coat
long before
she feels it bristle
knows the lovely lapping of his tongue
long before
she first feels his teeth
just a nip
between nuzzles
soon a nuzzle
between nips
frightened now
yet, the soft hunger remains
and she remains,
burying her face in his still-soft fur
while he feeds.

Believing his enchantment
may be broken through her own
she whispers
    even as his canines
sink
into her thin, bruised neck
while rich red flows
from her already empty heart
she whispers
as she closes her eyes
against his clear red glare
looses her grip
on his fathomless fur
whispers:

    "Oh, Grandmother! If you could only see ..."

Martha Miller

◆

An Unsent Letter

Dear Son,
   When you were a little boy and things were different with us, you used to climb on my lap every time I sat down. You were slender and your narrow butt fit in the rocking chair with me comfortably. You would kick at your brother if he came near, as if to say, this is my mom and my time, stay away. I remember you as a very blond, very angry child, who tested the limits of everything and who no one could handle but me. I went back to work when you were a baby. I remember waking you early in the morning, packing a diaper bag, and sending you and your brother, sleepy and full of fruit-flavored cereal and peanut butter, to a day-care center. When I picked you up at night we were all tired. Day after day droned on that way; I thought I would never get you to drink from a cup, never teach you to tie your shoes. Evenings our living room was always scattered with toys, the washer was always running.
   Sometimes I wonder what you remember of me from that time. I know you've told your counselors — not much at all. That I was never home. But I have pictures of us together. I can prove that our lives touched. And I know that every time I sat down, you climbed onto my lap. I would sit there, smoke cigarettes, drink tequila and press my nose in your dry, sun-bleached hair. You drew up your knees and folded into my arms. Until you were almost four years old you sucked your thumb. Everyone told me to break you of that sooner, but it was a comfort to you, and I had so little comfort to give.
   The day you asked if you could play T-ball, there were tears in your eyes. You could have asked for the world with that look and I would have tried to give it to you. I signed you up and saw to it that you got to your games. I remember the one I went to. I was impressed. You were good. I wish I would have come more.

I know I don't do as good as some parents. I also know I don't do as bad as others. I don't do as bad as the ones I had. I was the alcoholic daughter of an alcoholic father. I did not sober up until you were half grown. Long past your T-ball days, somewhere in the middle of Cub Scouts, I came home from the hospital with a clear head and found an angry little boy with a messy room who was always in trouble at school.

Your older brother was quieter and closer to his dad. You wouldn't let anyone close. I vowed to do better by all of you, but there were a lot of things about myself I didn't know. Less than two years later your father moved out of our home and a woman moved in. From then until the morning you ran away, I only remember a very rocky road for us.

I really wanted for us to be a family. I believed that was possible. I didn't understand anything about what was about to happen. I hung on and did the best I could. I fought your father, who tried to take you away from me. I fought with Suzie, who wanted me to let you go. And I fought with the rest of the world, who thought it was wrong for lesbians to raise children. Then I woke up one morning and your bedroom curtains were billowing inward. And your bed was empty.

When I first took Suzie as my lover it was a big adjustment. I don't think about it much these days. But it was painful at the time. We couldn't hold hands walking down the street. She couldn't put her arm around my shoulders in the theater. When the women at work talked about their husbands and boyfriends I sat quietly. Those sorts of sociological dysfunctions do something to a relationship. Lack of support and acknowledgement erodes the bonds. If validation is a kind of cement, it's no wonder lesbian relationships, on the average, are so short.

Suzie didn't like men. Here I was with two sons who were ready to enter adolescence, and I let a woman who felt that way into our lives and our home. I didn't see it then. That's my only excuse. She later turned out to be abusive to all of us. You and me and your brother. I watched you knock yourself out trying to make friends with her. Then I listened to her scream at me after you'd gone to bed, that I spoiled you, that I loved you more than her, that she hated you — would like to kill you. I tried to quiet her. You always claimed to not hear her tirades. You got so good at it, you managed not to hear my screams the night she tried to strangle me, during the last fight. Your room was ten feet away.

I am angry — at her and at me. Those were very hard years for us, dealing with her hostility at home and the hostility of the rest of the world outside of home. Later you told me, "Mom, I was just trying to survive with Suzie."

It is said that in ancient times gays were the chosen people. It was believed that we were closer to the gods because we lived in both worlds, male and female. But ancient times don't help me now.

Nor do they help you.

I told your brother that I was gay when he was twelve. I thought he was old enough to know. But you were younger. I figured I had a couple of years. Then I was cleaning your room and found a poem.

When I was a kid
at ten
My dad got divorced
he told me
That my mom was gay
And that was sad.
And now he has me pass
his joints all around
To Steve, and Del, and Jennifer . . .

I talked to you that night. I explained that all *gay* meant was that I loved Suzie the way I used to love your dad.

It was a lie. To you — and to me.

I really thought that that was all it meant.

As it turned out it also meant that the neighbors would throw trash in our yard, people would stare at us when we took walks in the evening during the summer, the neighbor's children would call us Homos, your father would hire a lawyer and try to take you both away from me, your brother would go live with him, and worst of all — your friends would tease you.

I think it's normal for kids at some point to be ashamed of their parents, but I handed it to you gift wrapped.

I remember pulling out of the driveway one afternoon. Our friend Stuart had been over. He had a new motor scooter and had given us all rides. You asked me, "Is Stuart gay?"

I said, "Yes. Beau is his lover."

You said softly, "Am I gay?"

I shrugged. "Probably not. Most people aren't."

I smiled to myself, thinking I handled that so well.

I should have pulled the car over. I should have embraced you. I should have offered you more comfort. Maybe at that point you thought gay was like the color of your eyes. Inherited. I could have told you that both my parents were straight and I didn't inherit that. I could have told you that being gay doesn't feel very strange. It's like having a different preference. It's liking chocolate ice cream when everybody else likes strawberry. It shouldn't make you a criminal, though in twenty-one states it does. It shouldn't make you lose your job, or lose your children.

Suzie had been gone for several months and I had met a new woman when you were fourteen, and ran away the first time. I was scared and angry. It was later that I saw the pure genius in your act, and I wished I could have gone with you. How many times had I felt like throwing a duffel bag in the trunk of the car and driving as far as the gas would take me?

I know you thought the new woman meant more abuse, even when I promised you I'd never let that happen again. I know you thought that, because with every new woman that followed you came a little more unglued. Maybe it wasn't just the abuse from Suzie that was too much — after all, she was gone. Maybe it was the added abuse from everyone around you that made it all unbearable. For many years all you said about my life-style was, "It's your business." The healthiest thing I ever saw you do was sit in a room with your counselor and a nurse on the psych ward (it took a fucking psych ward!) and tell me, finally, that you had some problems with my lesbianism. It was a hard thing for me to hear, but I knew you needed to say it, and deal with it. I wish I could have said, "If you have a problem with it, I will try to change." But that's impossible. Gay is not a choice. It's who I am.

In the long, long hours after I discovered you'd run away I wondered if you were dead or alive and if I'd ever see you again. Then you called me, told me what you had done and that you were coming home.

I said, "I'm coming to get you."

I took off work and left that night. For the whole long drive I was afraid. When I pulled into that little town in Arkansas and I saw first the car, then you, I thanked the God I had been praying to that whole trip.

Driving home, through Silver Dollar City and past Six Flags, I remembered all the times I told you we would take a trip together, all the times I'd gone without you because Suzie had insisted. The times I told you the car wouldn't make it, or we couldn't afford it.

You got your trip. The car made it.

I brought you home to a waiting police officer and handcuffs. I called the police because I saw the courts as a way to get the help for you that my insurance company had already refused to pay for. You were fourteen years old and out of control. You had stolen my car. I was afraid. I didn't know what else to do.

The day, sometime later, you told me you had a problem with my life-style, I was scared. It occurred to me that I could lose you. That you would go live with your father like your brother had.

I reluctantly offered.

You shook your head. "I don't even know him."

I waited, watching you.

"Mom, it embarrasses me," you said at last. "I've lost friends. I don't want to bring them home."

I nodded. I could believe it. The sun shone through the hospital window. Particles of dust swirled in the air. I remembered an old woman talking. "Gay life, now there's a funny word for it," she said. "It isn't very gay at all. Relationships are short. Society and your family reject you . . ."

One weekend, when you were about sixteen, you went with me to help my friends Cara and Kathy and their son Josh, who is just younger than you, to move. Several gay friends were helping. The man in the apartment next door was drunk. Josh came and told me that the man was shouting insults about dykes and lesbians.

I looked at him and sighed.

One of the men said, "I don't mind it for myself, but this is bad in front of the kids."

A painful knot tightened in my throat. How could he not mind? Are we so used to quietly sitting by that it doesn't matter? Have we listened to so many jokes in silence that we stopped feeling? Are we better at cowering under the abuse than taking what is rightfully ours? Or is it that we just don't know how? I've seen us in numbers, in parades, at music festivals — god, if we would just stand together. Just say, "Enough!"

"I'm calling the police," Kathy said.

I was scared then. I didn't want to deal with sneering police officers. But what else could we do? I thought the worst thing you could see us do was nothing. I wondered what you felt, tried to talk to you on the way home. You wouldn't discuss it.

It was several days later when Cara told me that you'd stood on the balcony and screamed, "Ignorant redneck!" And when the man tried to answer, you shouted, "Enough. I've heard enough!"

Sometimes I try to put it all together. Where we've been. Where we're going. This isn't what I thought raising a child would be like. I knew it took a long time and a lot of energy. I just didn't know that it took so long, and so much energy. I didn't count on things changing with me as much as with you. I didn't know what it would feel like to need to be a parent to you on days when I thought my own life was falling apart. You were in a lot of pain that I couldn't see during the divorce, during the years with Suzie, who was openly malicious toward you. You tried to tell me in your own way. But I had my own pain and couldn't hear.

When you and your brother were born, the one thing I knew about parenting was that I didn't want to make the same mistakes my parents made. And I haven't. I went out and found some new mistakes of my own.

I look at you now, a tall, blond, handsome young man whose smile does not come easy. Oh, I can still see your anger. And I know you've asked for many things I didn't give you. Knowing that, I send you this request. Down this long, long path of pain, I know that you have loved me. And I want for us to find a way to live together in quiet dignity, putting my many and your few mistakes in the past. I want this letter to be one last new beginning. A start of something right and strong between us.

Can we please both say, "Enough. We have hurt enough!"

I Love You,
Mom

Martha Miller

◆

Garden of the Hungry Cats

On the island of Malta, up the street from the British Hotel, there's a garden of statues called Barracca. It sits on the cliff overlooking the harbor. One of the American women hiked up there Sunday while the others were in church. She wanted to be alone. To think. To recover from the sting of Matty's words. It hadn't really been a quarrel, just a firm reminder.

She was the one who'd broken the rules. Matty had been sticking to the plan. But things were somewhat off balance. Askew. Regular customs and practices hadn't seemed to apply. Maybe it was the sun-bleached island in the Mediterranean, the hot wind from Africa that moaned like the Santa Annas for the first two days and nights, the ancient stone runes, temples of the goddess — Tarxien, Hagar Qim and Mnajdra — or the rotund stone figures of ancient women. Maybe it was the archaeological focus of the group of women they traveled with, the three witches from L.A., corn-fed, healthy looking women, who shared meals and buses but otherwise kept to themselves, the voices of the Italian women that floated up through the balcony window from the sun-bleached stone streets in the mornings, or the cats that screamed at night like women, breeding and hunting in the narrow alleys below. She'd never seen the sun so bright, glistening on the harbor like gold lamé — never missed diet soda and endless cups of coffee so much. Here images seemed backward, turned inside out, like a photo negative of possibilities, a picture where even the laws of nature had changed.

At sunrise she'd sat on the balcony and watched a pigeon roosting on the eaves, silhouetted against the blue and coral sky. She remembered the previous afternoon of sex in the primitive iron bed with squeaking springs. White sunlight had streamed through the windows. Sex had been slow, gentle and loving — without the desperation they felt in their limited time together back home. She'd lingered over Matty's triangle. Glistening black hairs as fine as silk. She'd pushed her tongue to dark salty regions, caverns of pleasure previously unexplored. Matty's fingers had left tingling trails of fire. Her touch was hypnotic. Enthralling. When they dressed for dinner she'd impulsively pulled Matty to her and said, "Leave him."

After an uneasy silence, Matty spoke softly into her shoulder. "You know I can't do that."

"We'll manage somehow."

"You left your husband for a woman, and she left you." Matty's accusation had trailed off.

Their eyes met. The air in the room seemed heavy and still. The woman dropped her arms and backed away nodding. Of course, nothing here could change the certain realities. Not even Malta.

The woman heard Matty stirring in the room behind her. She realized the roosting pigeon was gone, and wondered why she hadn't heard its flapping wings. She watched the sun continue to rise over the ocean. Small fishing boats made their way through the mouth of the harbor, moving slowly from a safe haven to the open sea.

After a while Matty said her name. The woman turned. Matty was dressed in her best black pants. A scarf covered her hair. "I'm going to church with the others. Are you sure you won't come?"

"I need some time alone."

Matty nodded.

The woman walked up the hill toward the garden. In front of the gate a black dog slept under a sign that said, "No dogs allowed." She took a picture. The paths were lined with dry bushes and palm trees. A round fountain trickled at the center. She looked out across the open sea to the place where it met the misty sky, then turned back toward the Valetta. She could see the hotel. Their room on the third floor, where a towel was drying in the balcony window.

A noise startled her. Close. Shrill. Like a woman's cry. She turned frantically. Saw nothing. The sound came again. She looked down. Just off the dusty pathway, a gaunt, gray cat lay under a dry bush nursing two small kittens. The cat looked wild. Hungry. She saw then that the garden was full of cats. Maybe the same ones she'd heard hunting beneath her windows at night. She remembered the dog laying patiently by the gate.

"You left your husband for a woman, and she left you."

Here in this beautiful city, this place rich with history and romance, there lived hundreds of starving cats. The garden was alive with them, under bushes, beneath the statues of the muses. As the woman strolled back toward the hotel she thought about Matty and sighed. She had paid so much, come so far, only to find this hunger.

Maria Mootry

◆

Poems

He's driving around town in her car

He's driving around town in her car
wandering on Wabash, cruising on Cook,
varooming down Veteran's.
"Lend me the key so I can get my tape," he'd said,
& like a fool she gave it to him.
Next thing she knew, he was gone.
She took one look: a blindingly beautiful day,
and 15-year-old hormones — go figure. It adds up.
"Fool," she muttered.

◆ ◆ ◆

So she calls a cab to her 11:00, sits back comfy
chatting with the driver about — what else —
15-year-olds' hormones.
Not bad. Being chauffeured; not having to drive.
But, he's driving around town in her car!
Rapping with friends, buying Buster Bars,
racing other cars!
Has he demolished an old lady yet? Flown through
Hometown Pantry's window? Gotten handcuffed by the police?

She bums a ride home with Pam — they talk about: what else?
15-year-olds & their hormones.
Not bad, a ride home, a chat on the front porch, advice,
while they wait for Pam's radiator to cool down.
Cool down! How can she?
He's driving around town in her car!
"It's about Power," Pam says. You betcha.
"I put mine's head through the wall," Pam says.
"You can't let them run your life," Pam says.

Oh, look, a note on the side door. He's been home.
"Me & J are driving around town in the car.
We're fine. Don't worry. See you later."
Oh, thanks a bunch.

"Call me and let me know how things turn out," Pam says,
lumbering off in her car.
She goes in, types, reads, eats, phones, anything to keep
from remembering, *he's driving around town in her car.*
His friends call. "He's not here, *he's driving around town*
in my car," she says. "Cool," they say, then, "Click."
Two hours into the evening the phone rings.
"Yo, Ma. We're at Hometown Pantry. Everything's fine.
Can we get you anything?" "No," she says.
Thinking, *Only a big ball and chain.*
"Come home," she says, "but don't rush."
She thinks: *You might kill yourself, your friends,*
and Lord knows who else.

Pam calls. "I told him not to hurry," she says.
"Mistake," Pam says. "You shoulda told him you'd have
the police on his ass and get home fast."
O.K. So nobody's perfect.
He's still out there, a public menace. The phone rings.
It is Josh, a friend. "No he's not here," she says. *"He's*
driving around . . . what did you say? He's walking into your
house now? Well tell him" (Oh what should she tell him to
tell him? Confusion, thy name is 15-year-old hormones!)
"Tell him he should get home by dark." She hangs up.

No, she doesn't want a 15-year-old public menace driving
around town after dark in her car. But it's getting dark.
She calls Josh's house. "Tell him he can stay there
till 10," she says.
*I can walk the four blocks to Josh's house
in no time,* she thinks. She throws on a jacket.

Outside, a dark night. September-fresh. Lovely.
Beats driving a car. Why hasn't she done it before?
Just — walk. Kids gather, talking softly on corners.
Dark, leafy trees. Cool cobbled streets. And there is Josh's
house. Sure enough, *he's* coming down the stairs. She can see
the key glistening in his hand. She sidles up to him and his
friend. She does not see her car. *He's been driving around
town in her car,* but where is it? "Where's the car?" she asks.
"It's over there," he says proudly, pointing to a
parking lot. He's walking fast, heading to the car, key in
hand. She wants her key. She wants her car, before he goes
driving around town in the dark; before 90,000 police
descend and make grass of his 15-year-old a - - .

"Give me the key," she says softly. He clutches it.
With a 15-year-old pouty sound he says, *"You said I could
drive."* She said no such thing, but she isn't about to argue.
Would he bolt like a colt? Would he run and jump in the car
and take off? She can feel him groping, thinking . . .
He swings around and faces her, hands her the key.

◆ ◆ ◆

They walk to the car. Inside it smells of teenage male cologne,
cheap smells for pimply girls.
Inside it is warm and comfy. She can feel that the seats have
been arranged. *Somebody else has been driving around
town in her car!* She slides behind the wheel.
"Don't ever do this again," she says, easing off.
"I'll call the police and report the car stolen, you hear? You
had me worried sick, *driving around town in my car!"*

Looking for Langston

Looking, looking for Langston, looking:
went to the river but the river was cold
chilled my body but not my soul
looking, looking for Langston, looking.

Ohio River was deep and wide, trying to get over
   to the other side:
looking, looking for Langston, looking.

"I saw Langston down on the levee"
"I saw Langston heading for Chicago"
"I saw Langston lighting out for St. Louie"
looking, looking for Langston, looking.

Hear that voice riffing on the wind
wind outta Kansas saying "my friend,
why you looking, looking for Langston? looking?
wind outta Harlem, wind outta Dakar, wind outta Paris
riffing, "homegirl, why you looking for Langston?"

"I saw Langston in the Hay Homes"
"I saw Langston over on the Southeast side"
"I saw Langston in Evergreen Terrace" Yeah!
"I saw Langston with the po' folks, no folks,
   underclass, no-counts, over-counts"
damn, Langston got more sightings than Elvis!

Looking for Langston in Lincoln, Illinois

at the Lincoln parade, we looked for Langston
in his old hometown
thinking he'd revisit shops, streets, alleys
where he walked into early manhood

we looked for Langston
under Orion's light
high school bands highstepped
round the city courthouse
blurting "i'll be home for xmas
if only in my dreams"

we looked for Langston
toetapping to bugles, drums, flutes,
saxophones, tubas, trumpets, french horns,
& flinging his arms wide in some place
in the night

past silos' long shadows
black against amber sun
glinting against umber soil
brushbrown trees
we strode the equipment bus
looking for you, Langston

isolated farmhouses
hugged the ground
windowpanes glinted reflecting falling sun
night came tenderly blacklikeyou

we looked for Langston
in every face straining to see
youths marching round the creamy domed courthouse
weary blues of the Christmas season
chased by eager chimes flowing round the town square
notes like a river you've known

we looked for you, Langston
jingle bell rock and holly jolly xmas
rang in the crisp air

we looked for you, Langston
and found you sauntering in and out between ghosts:
Brigham Young, Elijah P., Old Abe,
Grant, stamping on old stomping grounds.
We looked & found you, Langston
laughing & sharing a Tootsie Roll with a big-eyed boy.

Langston at Dakar: Presence Africaine

Long you stood
on the barracuda'd coast
of Dakar, Langston,
hand raised, shielding eyes
from Africa's black'ning sun;
you puzzled interstices,
"Bitter yearnings,"
"I am the darker brother,"
"What is Africa to me?"
"So long, so far away,"
"Night coming tenderly."

Now, dreams no longer deferred,
boys, idling on the beach
beseech pens from your
bulging pockets.
Turning, you hear a voice:
"Femme noire, femme obscure!"
You call back: "When Susannah wears red!"
Diasporic voice! Leopold
grasps your hand, leads you,
nimbly over burning sands,
to his big white castle;
behind you two, a legacy,
budding Achebes, Soyinkas,
scribbling furiously the future.

In a Dialogic Mode
(Deloria & Friends Talk)

The Lady Friends:
   "Now Deloria
   we know you 37 going on 67
   & that sweet sweetback of yrs
   aint even 40
   but it don't make no never mind
   all of us know you think you fine.
   & we younger than you
   but we wasnt born *last night,* you know.
   what you say
   if we say we saw Arletta coming
   out your house last night
   after you left for the AA meet?
   What you say for yourself, girl?"

Deloria's talkback:
   "Girls, I got to get up on this one.
   Now lemme tell you . . .
   I know you wasnt born last night
   & I know that heifer snuck to my house
   said she wanted to fix his hair
   & he let her in, he let that so & so in
   my house
   but girls, lemme tell you,
   I aint no pushover, you know that.
   If you act like a rug you get stomped on
   for shure.
   But to my mind it's like this:
   Honey, let me just *tell you,*
   Deloria just plain *too old to kill.*
   You hear me! Just *too old to kill* . . . "

At the Kitchen Table My Aunt Jean Confesses

Since u asked me, I'll confess. But I aint repentin' tho.
Yeah, baby, I love my food.
Smells, like a melody drift into my mind
of sweet corn, buttered . . . tomatoes, steamed . . . with okra,
porkchops and peppercorn, brown gravy,
butterdripping mashed potatoes.
Hmm-hmmmm.
And don't forget those greens: collards, mustard, turnips,
sweet with hocks and hot with Louisiana Red.
No Ma'am, I aint ashamed.
Smoked ham, sliced in hunks, not thin, honey.
Remember that song? *"Big fat Mama, meat shaking on her bones.*
Every time she walk by, a skinny woman lose her home."
That's me.
Just kiddin'.
Said I likes food, dont go round stealing other women's husbands.
Lemme see: macaroni with cheese, peach cobbler with white cream,
cornbread . . . all with lotsa *butter!*
I takes my choice: green beans, green peas, blackeyed peas!
Pecan pie, chess pie, blueberry pie, blackberry pie . . .
All with *butter,* lotsa butter.
Now they say butter's not good for you,
but I say folks gotta live till they die.
If I dont eat what I want, I may not live to be a hundred and ten,
but I'll sure feel like it!
Gimme a piece of that fresh corn on the cob, Alyce, and put lotsa
butter on it.
I thank u honey. Lord knows. You's a woman after my own heart.

Ginny Lee, Photographer

Ginny Lee keeps a light touch:
It's, "Hi there. When?
Tomorrow? Next Wednesday?
O.K.! Let's do it!"
Ginny Lee lives for chiaroscuro,
epiphanic moments:
O yes yes yes!
Let's get that earring spangling dazzle.
Now, don't blink! Blink!
Click!
I'm nailed forever.
(A better, photogenic me, a me I
never knew):
"Oooo Ginny, girl, never knew I could look
soooo good!"

To Gwen, Painter of Words

Priestess, portraitess, painter of words.
You caught us in all our postures:
The costumes, cosmetics and shifting architecture of our days
    across your unfolding canvas marched
Chocolate Mabbie & Pearl May Lee, Annie Allen & Big Bessie
Lester, Pee Wee, Satin-Legs & Alfred, the poet warrior.
All those moments of ennui, of confusion, of pain, of defiance.
The black and tan and yellow of it.
You liked the crush, the concentration of words (you said)
As painters love tempura's varied textures, water color's
    transparency, the opacity of oils.
And you did it.
You fixed us, at once inside and outside History.
Our images frozen in protean patterns
Forever negotiating between imagination and reality.
A lilting, luminescent, longlived legacy.
The signature, your brushwork words.

The Rest of the Story

Nobody ever told me the rest of the story —
All I remember is you standing in the doorway,
The bloodied panties crumpled around your left ankle,
The tears in your eyes,
And us, speechless, watching you cry,
Watching the burly police in the doorway, half-laughing
When you explained about the boy who did it.

Nobody ever told me the rest of the story,
How he took you to the building's top floor
Where his friends waited to take turns,
Wanted to have their way,
While you shook and cried on the concrete roof.

Nobody ever told me the rest of the story,
Why one of them changed his mind, said, "Enuf's enuf,
Let her go, she's rabbit-meat,"
And pushed you tearblinded, bleeding toward the stairwell.

Nobody ever told me the rest of the story, until now:
And I don't know whether to scream or say "thanks,"
For the one boy who raped you, then interceded,
And let you live to grow up & marry & have children.

And now, to look at you, the world, too, will never guess
The rest of the story.
All they will ever see is pools of sadness
In your big beautiful eyes.

Peg Knoepfle

───◆───

O Deer

I seem to have an obsession with antlered animals. Maybe I got it from my great-great-grandmother Brigid Goggin. She came over from Ireland and brought her seven children over, working as a dairy maid. It took her 19 years. She told her daughters, "Don't name your girls after me. In the United States, Brigid is just a servant's name." In Ireland it's the name of a saint or a goddess. So maybe I'm haunted by memories of the gods of Ireland, like the antlered god who is the messenger between the world of people and the spirit world.

Or maybe it's because of Revis Prairie in Mason County where I count butterflies and chop shrubs. The ravines at Revis are dark and deep and leafy. It's easy to get lost in them. When I'm lost, which is often, I look for deer trails to show me the way. I rejoice that they have been there before me.

The name of this story is "O Deer." It is a true story.

There was this tribe. They counted everything by deer. It was like the Eskimos having a hundred words for snow. But these people went further. Nothing was spoken of except in the context of deer. Zero was 0-deer. One was 1-deer. Blue was deer-standing-against-the-sky-on-a-nice-day. Red was deer-blood. A centipede was long-deer-with-100-short-legs. A sheep was a fuzzy-deer. Humans were deer-standing-upright. It took them hours to say anything. A fish was deer-nose-swimming-in-water. Trees were antlers-with-leaves.

The other tribes stopped trading with them. They thought all they had was deer. These people called diamonds transparent-deer-teeth. Who wants deer teeth? The people became backward. They couldn't talk fast enough, couldn't think fast enough.

Some stopped talking altogether. They only came out to the edge of the forest in the evening. Their friends called to them, but they wouldn't answer. Their children hid in the tall grass all day. After a while the only way you could tell them from deer is that they still had fingers. Others began to borrow words from different tribes just to get along. Learning new, fast words, they forgot the old ones. The old dances too. Their thoughts changed, though they still tended to mate in the fall. You see, they had lost their center. The heart-of-the-deer or deer-hart, as it was called. So they disappeared. It was either the woods or the marketplace.

Could it have been any different? I don't know. Obsessions are dangerous. But the problem here was language. They needed a story that runs along ridges, steps under branches into ravines, drinks from the river, wallows on the bluffs. They needed a wordless place to leave their deer shit. And I mean leave their deer shit. A place where no one dares to go, where they have always been.

Not everyone's lucky. Look for big-eyed children born in June or July. Look for palm prints on the deer trail. Look in the mirror.

Peg Knoepfle

◆

Poems

Letter to My Daughter

I will write you about each thing that makes me cry
because if it makes me cry, it's worth writing about.
That is the authority I have. Why record it if it's
worthless? Tears have substance.
I weep. Therefore I write.
I tell this to myself. I tell this to you.

And I did weep when I arrived at the demonstration
lining up, already lined up on the green grass
in front of the Illinois National Guard Headquarters.
It was March 21, 1987. We always need dates.
You know that and I do too. We're both journalists.

Coming towards me across the grass was a woman.
She was slim and slight, her hair faded to gold,
and I thought, "It's my mother" — your grandmother.
But of course it wasn't.

And indeed I never marched with my mother.
I was not in front of the State Capitol in Sacramento,
Ronald Reagan's guards up on the roof with their rifles.
I was not with Cesar Chavez.
I did not bring blankets for the Farmworkers
or gather baskets of pears for the Senior Gleaners.
I was not in the peace demonstrations
or the tutoring program.
I did not sit at the card table in the hot sun.

So it was only when I was standing on the green grass
in front of the National Guard gates that I saw
how she must have looked to another woman
in the late 1960s, the early 1970s, walking across
a California lawn, carrying a poster
perhaps like the one I had in my hand
with the names on it of people who had been killed.

And although tears came easily to her
especially for her own mother whom she lost young,
she did not need them to justify her life
or to prove the worth of anything.
That was a given with her.

So I stood next to my friend Lynette
and we shouted in our good Spanish
"No pasarán," as though we were at a football game.
Only we were not the type.

And our government
sent the Illinois National Guard
to help build the road from Tegucigalpa
to the Nicaraguan border. And our government said
the road was for "economic development."
But we said our government lied
and we called on the telephones day and night,
and Congress did not pass the bill for aid to the Contras.

And up on the roof of the National Guard Headquarters —
a student who'd been in the Guard told me this later —
they were carrying M-16s,
so it was
not so different from California after all.

And Lynette and I left, but we will also come back.
We are more the type than they think.

Position Title: Clerk Typist II
Position Number: 0845-04-50-000-10-01

i
up against a wall
a cream-colored wall
face to face
the wall doesn't have any face
it flattens the lens of my eyes
makes the rods and cones discouraged

ii
fingers on a typewriter
like walking on japanese stepping stones

but the keys sink some
and don't take me across the water

iii
the carpet is green
layered under each desk
with dust from phallic electric erasers
the carpet is office
augmented with coffee stains
crumbs from sue's swedish cookies
bookkeeping's melocreme donuts
peanuts from the midway pub
it reminds me of a church floor
hours spilled by the faithful
a place you go because you have to

iv
each one's body slants
a different way
into the work
the only angles I don't know
are my own

v
gloria says is he mentally ill?
max says not more than anybody else
max is going to burn his old sofa and his old rug
in a giant bonfire
gloria has waded in the waters of enlightenment
at virginia beach
max is wearing his bicentennial ac/dc tee shirt

thelma's purse so far
contains salt pepper needles thread mustard empirin
and freshly taken photos of the tower of pisa
we have not yet voiced all our needs
but are confident the purse
will rise to the occasion

vi
nance has made 100 pots
she has an earth glaze
grooved for the finger tips
and a gray mist fixed in fire
that can hide you from
the eye of mordor
but frodo is gone
he is lost
in the lost caboose trailer court
without a phone
where they cut cocaine
there is no clay to shape this story

vii
ferns breathe
leaves flare
in this house of clerks

viii
under the big tent
that the rain comes through
trapeze artists in moth-eaten blue velvets
get ready for the leap

Rosemary Richmond

Saab Story

On December 10, Ellen discovered that the bag lady had been sleeping in her car. Before that discovery, there had been telltale signs. The smell, for one. Ellen's old Saab smelled like a rat had died underneath the seat. Once Ellen had found a dead rat in the alley, by her garage. It was frozen. Ellen checked on the rat daily, looked at it from a distance. Finally, she threw dead leaves and a clump of dirt on the rat so she wouldn't have to look at it anymore. Once, a neighbor in the basement apartment had found a rat in her chest of drawers. Ellen thought about rats a lot. They frightened her. She could not understand how people could watch movies about rats, movies like *Ben* and *Willard*. To Ellen, rats were scary enough. She wondered if the bag lady was afraid of rats.

In order to get the rancid smell out of her car, Ellen paid five dollars to have it cleaned. If there truly was a rat under the seat, she didn't want to be the one who found it. But the guys at the car wash didn't find a dead rat under the seat. They found pennies, paper clips, dustballs, paper, broken pens.

Two other clues alerted Ellen that the bag lady was using her car. The driver's door was ajar and a package was placed on the passenger's seat. It was wrapped neatly in newspaper as if it were a Christmas present. Ellen unwrapped it and found two packages of cigarettes: Virginia Slims. One package was open. Ellen tossed the package in the garbage can before she realized who it might belong to. Later, she checked the trash can to see if the package was still there. It wasn't.

Ellen knew about the bag lady. In an odd way, Ellen admired her. The bag lady managed to live without buying things she couldn't afford. The bag lady didn't measure her worth in terms of accomplishments and possessions. She was doing what most people were doing: getting by the best way she knew how. Living not on the edge, but over it.

In the summer, the bag lady had been arrested for throwing rocks at the young boys who taunted her. Ellen had learned the bag lady's name by reading it in Police Beat. Daisy Buckman was her name. The name reminded Ellen of Daisy Buchanan from *The Great Gatsby,* F. Scott Fitzgerald's novel. This Daisy was nothing like the one in the book. In Fitzgerald's story, Daisy was soft, blonde, golden, rich. This Daisy was hard, grey, brittle, poor. Her name should have matched her looks, Ellen thought. Daisy's name should have been Maude or Beulah.

Daisy fascinated Ellen. She walked through the alley behind Ellen's apartment building smoking, muttering, cursing. The neighbors gossiped about the way she cussed, her vulgar language. Her curses frightened them: horrible words, streamed out in a cadence, a rhythm, like a poem gone bad.

Like Daisy, Ellen cursed too. A lot more than she liked. It concerned Ellen that she loved the language so much and abused it so frequently. Every New Year's she resolved to clean up her garbage mouth. But the use of the "F" word had become habitual and she used it again and again, unconsciously. Trying to stop cursing was like trying to stop smoking, Ellen thought. She had to remain conscious of her behavior and it was too much work.

From Ellen's window, she could watch Daisy cursing at people from long ago. In the mild weather, she would sit at the picnic table outside the convenience store. Daisy seemed to hold conversations, shaking her finger at imaginary foes, cursing. From both her verbal and nonverbal communication, Ellen knew that Daisy was angry to the bone. In a way, Ellen envied her. At least Daisy was getting her anger outside of her now. Ellen's anger accumulated like her unpaid bills.

Daisy hung out in the garages behind Ellen's apartment building. There was a long row of them. Since Ellen had never seen Daisy in her garage in the daytime, she assumed Daisy wasn't interested in using her garage. Other neighbors had caught Daisy in their garages. One of them yelled at her, threatened her. Later, the neighbor told Ellen she didn't want Daisy in her garage. She was afraid Daisy might urinate in it. Ellen didn't worry about that. But she didn't have a new car, either. The other woman did.

If Ellen had had her dream car, an '88 Saab, she would not have liked Daisy sleeping in it, stinking up the smell of new leather. But then, if Ellen had had a new Saab, Daisy probably would not have been able to get into it. Ellen would have been able to lock the doors of her Saab. The car she now owned did not have door handles. Only the driver's side opened. To enter the car, Ellen had to insert a long screwdriver into the hole where the handle had been and then push. Ellen kept a supply of screwdrivers in the trunk for this purpose. The trunk didn't lock either. Did Daisy know this? Had she, in fact, watched Ellen?

Ellen debated what to do about the problem. On the one hand, Ellen worried that Daisy might oversleep and she might find her in the car. She had heard that Daisy was mean, and in a way Ellen was afraid of her. Daisy was no longer in touch with reality and those kinds of people scared Ellen. Ellen had known too many people like Daisy and the effect they could have on her. Ellen felt sorry for them and they knew it.

Ellen told her kids about the bag lady using her car. Her son said once Daisy had politely asked him to bring her packets of sugar from the corner White Hen, which he did. Ellen's daughter raged. She worried that Daisy might try to get into her new car which was occasionally parked in Ellen's garage. Ellen found herself defending Daisy, saying that she was not a thief. She would not break and enter. She would not steal. Ellen kept shoes in her back seat, good shoes. They were never missing. Ellen thought if Daisy would want to steal anything it might be shoes. "Daisy does not steal," Ellen told her daughter, "she borrows." Still, Ellen's daughter did not relent. She accused Ellen of feeling sorry for everyone, of identifying too closely.

The truth was, Ellen worried about becoming a bag lady. She collected shopping bags from Saks Fifth Avenue, Bergdorf Goodman, Macy's. If she were to become a bag lady, she would be fashionable. She would carry the best bags in town. She wondered how many bags she would need to carry her prized possessions around with her. In the end she would probably dump them all, like Daisy, and settle for carrying a package of cigarettes in her pocket.

For Christmas, Ellen bought Daisy a package of McDonald's coupons. She wrapped the package in brightly-colored Santa Claus paper and left it on the passenger seat where she had found the cigarettes. She also left a sleeping bag in the backseat. She wondered if Daisy would cover with it.

As a Christmas present to herself, Ellen considered ordering two door handles for her Saab. She talked with her mechanic who said they would cost about one hundred dollars apiece and that price did not include installation. Installing the door handles would be expensive, he said, because the locks were broken. It would take six weeks to get the door handles. Did she want to order them, her mechanic wanted to know. Ellen said she'd think about it.

Rosemary Richmond

Poems

The Pause in Between

She used to have a period but
now she has a point of exclamation!
She used to have a period but now
she is like a comma, pausing, pausing,
no complete stop she used to have
a period but now she has a swollen
    semi-colon

she used to have a period but now
she feels like a dash — punctuated
and mechanically correct — an
informal mark.

Time

Those early morning
hours wait patiently
like a mother
hands circle wide like a dancer.
They seem not to
cry, but to whisper gently
oh use me — write.

Bad Blood

I. She is your sister.
Her red cells are destroying white cells.

A doctor calls from Chicago, tells you she is dying.
"In an emergency measure, we removed her spleen."

When you arrive she tells you she is not dead yet.

You stay all night in a hotel with your older sister: she gets crabs and you do not.

Your sister lives but doctors do not know why.

"An allergic reaction to Nyquil," they say.

Twenty-seven years later you want your sister to buy life insurance. The company says, "Extensive Bloodwork Required." Your sister refuses.

II. He is your son, your youngest child, born red but turns chalk-white-blue.

You take him to six doctors in six weeks. A doctor orders a blood count and sends him to the hospital for a transfusion.

"His hemoglobin dropped. We don't know why. We're lucky he's alive. One more week and he would have been dead."

He is pink but not whole. At twenty-three, he can't read.

You find out he has extra pieces on six pairs of chromosomes. You puzzle over the connections.

III. She is your older sister. She has three cancers: spinal column, bone marrow and blood. Multiple Myeloma: a rare form of blood cancer that occurs in blacks more than whites, men more than women. Your sister is white.

You pray for her to live and prepare for her to die.

Vicki Bamman

───◆───

Poems

I don't understand why we're friends

I don't understand why we're friends.
You never flatter me
    and you never believe any of the illusions
    about myself that I construct.
You never let me lie to myself
    and you never hesitate to criticize,
    being more honest with me
    than I am with myself.
You tease me
    and you believe in me
    with a faith that I lack.
I don't know what you see in me
    but I admire you
        extravagantly.

Remember the night we sat late at Rank's,
    talking too much
    and drinking,
and saying things we never say when we're sober.
You said I was charming.
    I've always wanted someone to say that,
    did you know?
I looked for the right good words for you,
    and you said there aren't any.

There are:
You're my friend, and I love you.

Days, weeks, months pass
between calls,
and we never write
but you always seem to come
    when I need you most.
Sometimes you need me too,
    to listen to you,
    to laugh with you,
to hold your hand when you're hurt.
I'm on your side and you're on mine.
You're open and honest and caring and kind,
and — yes, I'll say it —
you're charming too,
    and most of all you're fun.

I remember the Christmas
you gave me a fruitcake
    with a note that said
      "Sweets for the sweet"
and I gave you a box of nuts
with the same message.

Great friends with a single thought.

The Interview

Black dress and pearls
mask of makeup
on high heels I tiptoe

You men,
striped suits and ties,
flirtatious eyes,
ask your hard questions
but you don't hear me answer.

Someone else,
taller and thinner than I
gestures with my hands
speaks with my voice

Rage

Suddenly
it's there again,
tightening the muscles in my throat.
Words rasp out harshly
in a voice almost strangled at birth.
    It crawls
under the skin of neck and shoulders,
raising prickles of hair.
Animal ancestors bared their teeth too.
It fills my chest until
there is no room for breath
    or blood.
It radiates invisible arrows of red and violet
that stab and prick anyone who comes near.
It seeps from my breasts,
poisoning the air before me.
I can nurture nobody,
clasping only emptiness to myself.

The flowers on my desk are dying

The flowers on my desk are dying.

The snapdragons still snap,
    but weakly,
feel like velvet to my touch.
Their color has deepened
    to rich shades
    of wine
    and purple.

The rose is fully blown,
its golden heart exposed.
The petals curl,
the colors fade,
    ivory
        edged and tipped with pink.
The texture is like the cheek
    of an old woman
    who has known tears
and
    love.

Can you hear me?

I speak slowly,
    with emphasis
      pushing
          my words
              toward you.

You wait

for

    something
    to reach you.

My words are

    lost
in the
    space
        between

us.

Can't you hear me?

The merry-go-round

The merry-go-round creaks.
Jeff's feet patter in the dust,
making little puffs, cartoon-like.
He pushes the merry-go-round,
jumps on, drags his toes as he spins.
Little round Amanda
in too-small shorts and too-large shirt
leans against the bars of the merry-go-round.
She smiles at the blurred playground
as she wheels past me.
In the middle of the merry-go-round,
Tiffany sits, legs spraddled out.
Hands cling tightly.
Her dress is ruffly and dirty,
party clothes rolled in dust.
Sneakers too big, legs too thin,
eyes large, beautiful, solemn.
She doesn't smile.
Another girl calls her poopy-pants.
She doesn't respond.

Debi Sue Edmund

◆

Back Talk

But what do women want?

Equality.

Oh, I'm not one of those feminists. I like men.

I like men too. And I *am* a feminist.

Don't feminists hate men?

The fact that I consider myself to be their equal does not mean that I hate men or boys, or that I want to hurt them. What I do hate are certain attitudes. Together with others, I am working to change laws, social customs, values and institutions that hurt women and girls.

Feminists are anti-family.

Feminists are "pro" all kinds of families. Single-parent families and stepfamilies as well as the more "traditional" model. Families with women who earn an income as well as families with a mother who stays home with her children. Families from all races and ethnic backgrounds. Families with elderly people who live on a fixed income as well as young families. In other words, feminists want to see our society be more supportive of *all* families. Not just those who match the stereotype we see on *Father Knows Best* or *Leave It to Beaver* reruns.

What do the women's libbers have against motherhood?

Not a thing. Lots of feminists *are* mothers. However, we don't believe women's choices should be limited to marriage and motherhood. Our society doesn't expect men to sacrifice all their hopes and dreams and career ambitions as a price tag for having children, and we shouldn't expect it from women either. Furthermore, it's time we stop encouraging women (or men) to feel like unnatural freaks if they don't — or can't — have children.

Working mothers look down on mothers who choose to stay home with their children. Feminists are to blame for that.

Feminists were the first to point out, "All mothers work." You won't hear *us* asking a woman who's done ten loads of laundry and chased a toddler around the house, "What did *you* do all day?" We have fought for laws that take the true economic and social value of homemaking and childrearing into consideration when determining retirement benefits, divorce settlements or welfare eligibility. That said, it's way past time to stop making mothers who work outside the home feel guilty about their decision, and blaming them for everything that's wrong with our society.

Now they look down on women who work at "traditional jobs" such as waitress, housekeeper, nurse or teacher.

For years, feminists have argued for "comparable worth" policies. We believe that jobs traditionally held by women should be valued as highly as jobs traditionally held by men, and that paychecks should reflect this. Why should the job titles "housekeeper" and "janitor" have different pay scales when both involve the same kind of work?

I hired a woman once and she just didn't work out. So naturally, the thought of another hiring decision like that one makes me nervous.

Did you ever hire a man who didn't work out? After that happened, I'll bet you told yourself, "I'll never do that again."

White males are becoming an endangered species.

We are not seeking to rid the world of white males. We are simply saying the world doesn't revolve around them.

The problem with today's women is, they expect to have a career and *a marriage* and *children. They want it all.*

Men have always counted on having a career *and* a marriage *and* children. Yet we don't hear folks whining about the selfishness and irresponsibility of men who "want it all."

Feminists want women to dominate men.

Feminists want women and men to be equal. That means nobody dominates anybody else.

Seriously, strong women threaten the fragile male ego.

Certainly we should treat men, as well as women, with dignity and respect. But we can respect others without putting ourselves down — which is what we do when we simper, snivel, play dumb, deny our own abilities and grant more worth to someone else than we grant to ourselves. Respect is not synonymous with boot licking. It's time the myth of the fragile male ego went the way of the chastity belt.

Women who refuse to play the female role are not only unfeminine, they're unnatural.

I'm a human being living a life, not an actor or robot playing a role. Besides, if submissiveness and all those other "feminine" traits are so natural, why does our society have to bully so many women into adopting them? Women would just do these things "naturally," wouldn't they?

Face it, even today, some boys don't like a girl who is too smart.

Boys with this attitude are assuming that a smart girl would want *them*. That's an amazing assumption.

Feminism was established so unattractive women could have easier access to the mainstream.

Yes, and isn't that wonderful? We've discovered that female beauty comes in all sizes, shapes, colors and ages. And once we stop subjecting ourselves to an impossible one-size-fits-all standard, some of us are amazed and relieved to discover that we aren't ugly after all.

Feminists encourage women to be lesbians.

Feminists encourage women to be themselves. For about three to ten percent of women, that *is* lesbian.

The average feminist is sexually frustrated. One good f— and she'd be whistling a different tune.

Hmmmmm. Wishful thinking?

Next thing you know, we'll have unisex bathrooms.

Feminism has been around for several decades now and I'm relieved to report "Hers" and "His" public restrooms everywhere I go. (Good thing too. Who wants to wait in a long line when some of us can sneak into the other one?)

If we get rid of gender roles, our identities will get all mixed up. How will we distinguish the male from the female?

If you have a penis, you're male. If you have a vagina, you're female.

What about opening the door for a woman? Are these little courtesies dead?

Common courtesy is always appropriate. By all means, open the door for a woman (or man) whose arms are full. And while you're focused on opening doors, how about the doors that lead to the executive suite and the board room?

Do you have to be so shrill? So strident?

If you listen to me the first time, I promise not to shout. Or repeat myself like a broken record.

For women to be feminists, don't they have to stop wearing makeup and shaving their legs? What if they don't feel comfortable doing that?

Some feminist women shave their legs. Some don't. Some wear make-up and earrings. Some sport tattoos and pierce their belly buttons. Some wear long skirts, some wear miniskirts, some wear pants, some wear bras, some go braless and some would go skyclad if it were legal. One of the advantages of being a feminist is that I get to decide how I should look. I don't have to let someone else — including men or fashion designers or the advertising industry — dictate that to me.

I'm not sure I want to be associated with a bunch of bra-burners.

Last time I tossed a bra in the trash, the poor thing was too old and tattered to hold anything up. I bought some new ones.

But feminists are pretty radical.

Many ideas we calmly accept now — a woman voting in an election, a woman attending law school, a woman taking a birth control pill — were considered radical in our mothers' or grandmothers' day. We take these things for granted today, thanks to generations of feminist activism. It's really a sad commentary on our own times that full equality — and personhood — for women is still considered by some to be a radical notion.

If I believe in equal rights, can't I just say that? Why do I need to call myself a feminist? It has such negative connotations.

Of course, people should feel free to define themselves however they want to. But it's important that we not be afraid of that word, or opponents of equal rights will use our fear to push us right back into the bad old days. I like to repeat a quotation attributed to Rebecca West in 1913: "I myself have never been able to find out precisely what feminism is. I only know that people call me a feminist whenever I express sentiments that distinguish me from a doormat."

God does not like feminists.

Oh yeah? Who says She doesn't?

Why do you have to be such a bitch?

Me? I'm just getting started.

Kate Kanaley Miller

◆

Poems

this is the first tree
    the image made in likeness
    the red blood brown of leaf stains
    and human blood, sisters-brothers-
    of-being-rooted in the dark humus,
    humility of our former selves, ancestors
    of our own beginnings, leaves imprints,
    the skeleton of leaves, the veins of
    hands and fingers, of face, we are the tree
    inside, pushing the pain of our inability
    to move, but rooted, align ourselves to life,
    the light enwombed becomes healing wisdom,
    is born anew again, borne into the world
    our being true, the light courses like a heavy
    river in our bed of pain, keeping alive all
    meaning, drowning the rest, and praying, eyes
    closed, unmoving, we see and are moved, she
    turns her palms to the unknown and leaves
    hand prints

back to the tree

the beautiful flicker hit the plate glass
hard, with his head,
full force, flying
she watches his return to the tree,
slightly dazed

feathers stuck to the glass,
a huddle of testimony
she feels she should be able to go through
to pass swiftly, flying
is sure she has left pieces of herself
on this side

without walking

a tree gathers sun, catches
out of the wind,
minerals, and draws
up from roots
deep in darkness and humus,
pooled water of raindrops,
is content and grows; upon
this wooden bench, worn smooth,
in silence I let my deep light
speak

it's that uncluttered look I want

it's that uncluttered look I want
like when you just stepped into the room
after somebody moved out, the walls
empty of their adornments, fresh
easels to the mind; the mantel begging
for some primitive reminder of a more
ancient nature, when the odor of wood-
burning really meant something like life,
and warmth and survival. the floor empty
and carpeted, a room waiting for sitting
where, if you were not a little daft,
a television would talk to you,
against that wall, a desk,
across the room a cabinet for music.

I remember when it was new like that, before
the furniture, the candles, the angel,
extra rocks, and all the little things that fill up cracks
in our hearts, an electricity ran through,
buzzed around the room from empty place to
empty place. I danced in the expectant room,
danced that night the first full moon
shone through the new skylights, lay on
the floor then, moon bathed my way back to
somewhere before I was born.
with only a couch and a sleeping bag I moved in,
stole sleep from all those strange night sounds,
something would go wrong but it didn't.
a bed arrived for the upstairs, set by the window,
looked through the trees, but
I am not camping there.

After two years
I took down the angel, the candles, the
rocks, and all kinds of things that fill cracks,
begged the room to be empty again, it will take practice
to unfill a void, to let one lean idea scalpel
its way in, cut out expectations that clog the flow,
and allow my surgeon's hand to heal.

at the book store weeping words

I have come to sit among books
into a soft chair my body collapses,
such a gentle yielding even my bones relax,
eyes scan the shelves for names of friends,
"love, medicine and miracles"
alternative medicine to my left
bibles and nutrition on my right
ahead on a low wooden carved table
"feng shui: ancient oriental art"
"a soul in place: reclaiming home as sacred space"
"When Elephants Weep: The Emotional Life of Animals"
is my desk, holds the paper flat, stiff enough for writing,
it is I that am stiff, unable to spill words
from my sacred place where healing and miracles reside.

across town at the Book Fair earlier today,
all those authors, all the words they said,
"Do a chapbook," "that's nice; that poem is nice"
I heard them read their own work,
at times I did not know I was there
the words had put me inside of them
all I could do is hang on
how could this be, we were all sitting there
just listening.
later, she, the poet, tells me,
"it feels so good to read someone saying
what you have felt but never heard before,
you need to write about it, don't take too long,
don't become so distant. I write to save my life."

I cannot write for fear I will lose or loose
myself; but those footprints of spirit that got lost,
cry to come back, be identified, lead to something.
> *Emotional tears are different in that they*
> *contain a higher percentage of protein, the*
> *elephant book says. Darwin was unable to ob-*
> *serve animals shedding emotional tears and*
> *called weeping one of the special "expressions*
> *of man." It was reported by Sir E. Tenant*
> *that some newly captured elephants in Ceylon*
> *tied up and lying motionless on the ground*
> *showed "no other indications of suffering*
> *than the tears which suffused their eyes and*
> *flowed incessantly."*

but still I cannot tell you how it felt to wake in that bed
my hands tied to the rails, a breathing tube in place, no
one to talk to, no one to listen even if I could have spoken

recently the eye doctor said I had dry eyes, very dry
and so it was with no small joy I cried on Thursday,
no one could console me.
I had to admit to myself,
so hard it is to admit these things,
it didn't matter how much I had suffered,
nor whether I had bargained all my pain for their freedom,
my children and my grand children, would suffer their own
pain, even some of the same. I cried that whole morning
not wanting to be wrong.
If only I had not expected something different
than life it might not have been so sad,
if the pain had been too much
I couldn't tell of it
but now
the elephant has settled on my pen,
and still you do not
know me

Jesus coming to you altared

a candle burns, honors
this temple mirrored in me glowing,
we are meeting for the first
time as equals, I have finally
brought you down from the high
places I could not reach you,
namaste, to the Divine in you
from the Divine in me, energy
swirls, walk with me at the shore
through an ocean of meaning,
we can play now free in Elysian
Fields, clear the spaces in
synapses for connection, rejoice
with sympathy for each others pain,
and know the gifts of resurrection,
phoenix rising, ashes ashes everywhere
bells across a Sonoran desert
toll shivers of flame inward,
deeper, deeper, places of still pools,
altar yourself and know all is good,
even these deaths.

your eagerness to hear me

if I had not seen you earlier
I would not now be unable to sleep,
a winter night rich with moon
stalks my wakened loneliness, in letters
the slow undress of mask has hidden
desire, I see you alone in your house
across a town of barriers, sweet passion
whispers a prayer to the cold moon's ear,
an architect of dream in this year of your
mourning, sleep will not embrace a yearning
heart afraid of needing too

in-corporate

you look scared, locked in
yourself, behind the glass you
cannot feel safe in front of, I was
told to stand at a mirror, look into my own
eyes, say, "I love you," but
that deep eye unstable
stare imprisons the words somewhere
between speaking and dying, will not
penetrate, or take up living,
practitioners of affirmations say it
anyway, the self conscious utterings
of disbelief bypass hard-wired logic
fences, slip into believing, under,
below the formalities of truth
fulness and fill a sub
let soul.

that's all you have to do

how did life and love get
separated from living, and
words become lonely in language,
when did a black hole begin
walking, how did naked winter trees
become flags without breathing, and when did
everyone leave, and we become half of something

and how does a ray of sunshine light all that
dust, and sanctified moments make humaness
a crime, and what about all those times you
weren't taken in or fed, and why
do you wither in a warm house, and the
homeless laugh even once, sirens sound always
for someone else; is prayer enough

and what in common do you have with
the woman whose six children were tied to her
before she was thrown into the river, and the one
who was made to sit before the
oven while the soldiers placed her baby
in a baking dish, and the man in the camps
who lined up naked holding in papers his life grabbed
from him and torn into pieces which fluttered to the
ground at his feet, or the blind man who haunts the down
town with pencils, an accordion and bubble gum
who forty years ago smiled and said thank you
just as he did yesterday

and then the unexpected bird sings.

to Anne Frank

Sweet child, born
of dying, language
hurts so helpless
at tempting peace,
a sorrow all words
cannot swallow
a return, a blasphemy to
say sister, yet
we embrace wherever
innocence is
brutalized, and I say I am
sorry, but mean so
much
more

Hilda Beltran Wagner

How He Made Do

how could I forget the old man

his granddaughter had brought us milk
still hot from the cow's udder that morning
and in the evening he amazed us beneath a cherry tree

or how humid it was
branches drooping with fruit
roots grasping the ground
stretching unseen
east toward the Ukraine
west toward Warsaw
the unsteadiness

of the stool he sat upon,
of his fingers
as he fumbled through leaves
reached for one leaf,
plucked then creased that leaf
trembling the whole time

and how the leaf trembled too

when he brought it toward his lips
for a sudden kiss of music —
an unbelievable, outrageous, anachronistic purity of breath
transformed into melody creaky as wood
but complete with tone and vibrato and form

squeaky, for sure, but jazz nonetheless
    Summertime
(can you hear it?)
even now I hear myself
thinking right in rhythm
that history might as well stop
enough pompous percussion
we just want the music of trees
of old Poles mastering Gershwin — and on leaves!
strange places suddenly familiar
our ears filled with music
our bellies warm
and to believe
that *the livin' is easy*
you just make do

but he stopped cold right then
holding back as a redundant riff
burned along the horizon,
nodded his head, slapped his knee
paying respect to silent performance
the genius of heavy air
the skill of the sky waiting for darkness
the rain waiting to fall
the brilliancy of the gospel
Judas might have written
had he chosen instead to tell his tale

I lived
this is how
I entertained
first Hitler's troops
then Stalin's
it's good playing now
for some Americans

and with that, he played on
letting the long phrase of captive song
lift easily up
and float easily back
to the shivering shadow of tree it had come from
having saved no one, not even itself

Rena Brannan

◆

Monochrome

Jumble felt the speed fly up her nose. It tasted like a metal pan she once licked when she was a small child. That part of it wasn't too bad. The bad, painful part of crystal methamphetamine was the crystal. It cut into her tiny blood vessels, filled nostrils, one shot up the left and one up the right. It left her eyes ravaged. It sucked up all the Evian drinking days of her potable youth. It burned, baby. It burned like a demon's revenge through her sinus cavity. It burned like heaven through her small nose into her ever present large cerebrum attacking and attaching itself to several nerves and cells. It wasn't pretty, it wasn't clean and it wasn't healthy. Jumble knew all of that. Jumble knew exactly what the speed was doing to her at all times, besides chronic ear infections. (Which always prompted a Jumble memory whenever she thought about it. Knock, knock. Who's there? I cunt hear you I have an ear infucktion.) It also caused chronic sleep disorder, which she used to her advantage. Jumble was from the burn-bright-for-2-seconds-then-die crowd. She wanted to do it all. Surf the waves off the Malibu coast. Surf the net off the Global coast. Climb the Grand Canyon. Fuck her way to the top and back down again. She wanted to make things, and she did. She made things happen. Her best friend Jey was in jail. Everyone thought Jey was in for killing Jackson. But Jumble knew it had everything to do with the Ginsberg Soliloquy.

"He is waiting. He is not waiting. He has fucked. He has not fucked. Do you understand me? Present tense excluded." Jey spit and screamed and spit some more. "This is Ginsberg and this is my Soliloquy. I have his scalp in this jar. I am finished with waiting. I am finished with Godot. He is dead. Is he dead? God forgives those who are dead. Or is it whom? Howl you dumb sons-of-bitches."

Jumble watched as the coffee stained crowd inhaled the nicotine flavored mint chewing inside Jey's bleeding infected gums. They stood, they stumbled, then they pissed and howled all of them. Every one of them from the soft, sexy, kitten, howl, to the deep, knee, wolf howl, to the guilty, pleasure, parakeet, Jumble knew that this Ginsberg Soliloquy was not over and she feared for its solid carbon monoxide soul.

Jumble knew that she would have to go visit Jey. She sniffed up the other line, pressing her nose to the compact disc case, eye to eye with Regis Fillburn's greatest hits. He kind of reminded her of Dick Clark, creepy, ageless, and with strange hair. She thought that the Regis and Kathy Lee show was just a substitute *American Bandstand* for the nineties.

At twenty-nine she felt herself attached to the tentacles of pop culture and understood that Andy was still making art after his death. She felt that Warhol was looking down upon her flat two-dimensional life and guiding it with his thoughtless languid fingers. She had briefly met Warhol in 1969. Minutes before the famous disappearance of Billy Name, Jumble had been sucking at her mother's breast. Jumble had been in the throes of ecstasy. The kind babies get when the milk starts to trickle from nipple to mouth and their eyes roll back from the first heavenly doses of life. Jumble believed that most artificial food shapes resembled the breast and not the penis, but there was no way to prove it. Belief was such a specific thing and to most the penis came first and not the egg. She was in Billy's darkroom with her mother. Warhol had this thing about children and they weren't allowed in the Factory. Jumble's mother had been sneaking her in every day for several weeks. If Jumble's mother had been part of Warhol's coterie, it might have been an entirely different story. A story more about pictures than art, more about obscurity than text. A fifteen-minute story about a famous child breast-feeding in the Factory during the height of Warhol's descent. But really Jumble's mother was an afterthought. She hung around the scene. She was seduced by the glamour and she was paralyzed by the ugly confrontations. No one knew who she was but almost everyone believed she was Andy's cleaning lady. No one knew what Andy believed except Andy.

Then there was this strange story that circulated right after Andy's death from the nurse who said she had talked to him about her younger sister Nancy. Jumble had read about the nurse and Andy's conversation several weeks earlier on the Internet.

"Do you remember Nancy?" the nurse had asked Warhol.

Andy's reply intrigued Jumble. Warhol had told the nurse, "Sweetheart, we didn't go for dull names, although there was this woman who everyone thought was my cleaning lady. She stayed mostly in Billy's darkroom. I think Billy took one picture of her. I caught her breast-feeding. It was such an unlikely event. Oh God, breast-feeding in the Factory. I should have silk-screened her breast and my 'Don't Park Here' sign together. Oh well, she disappeared. I made everyone disappear, even Elvis once."

In the darkroom Jumble fed. She felt her mother clutching her. Then suddenly Jumble felt her mother's breast yanked out of her small baby slurping mouth. Jumble heard a noise and saw a shock of white hair. She remembered specifically, a crying sound. That was her very brief encounter with Andy.

Jey, oh God, Jey. Jumble had to go see Jey. It was a catastrophe that brought Jey and Jumble together. As Jey tells it, she was driving on the Santa Monica freeway going toward the ocean. She had gotten off right where the 405 and the 10 meet. It was one of Jey's favorite routes. No matter how out of the way it was, Jey always needed to take that exit, and she would make it work. Crisscrossing back over to Pico or Lincoln, she knew which way to go whether it was North or South, East or West, and if you were a passenger, she'd tell you how much shorter it was, until you were agreeing with her every turn. Jey was driving down the 10. She had her bullet in one hand and was stuffing it up her nose. Cocaine was Jey's addiction; maybe it was more an act of contrition. Everyone knew Jey was in A.A. and she loved the dogma. She could recite and flavor her testimony as if she had been sober going on fifteen years. Her friends thought she was straight except for her immense nicotine habit. Jey lived. Which was more than most people her age were doing. She spoke several languages. She wrote elliptical poetry, which she had conceived as a new poetic form. Jey was critical of traditional verse, and she was also critical of improvised form. She hated honesty, she hated informal, discursive, repetitive poetry, and she loved Ginsberg. She couldn't abide with such juxtaposed feelings. She often felt trapped. Her body was romantic. It liked soft cotton sheets, soothing oil and mineral baths. Soft candlelight. Her mind was another animal, another species altogether. Jey was narcotized as she hit the bullet again. She felt as if the car was her body. Then Jey accelerated into the car stopping in front of her. She didn't know why she had stomped down on the accelerator. Jey knew she hadn't seen the other car until she hit it. It was the back of Jumble's Toyota that Jey hit.

Jumble was glancing at the *L.A. Times* when she noticed that traffic was slowing. As she came to a full stop, she felt herself jolt against the seat belt and flop back into her seat. It was the first time in months where anything felt slow. Jumble's eyes were stinging. She rubbed them. "Don't rub your eyes," her nonexistent mother would chant. Her eyes felt thick and slimy. Jumble kept blinking. Her eyelashes seemed sticky. It became harder and harder to open them. It reminded her of a Venus flytrap, except she didn't really want to know what she was attracting. Then she passed out.

"You crazy bitch," Jey screamed at the woman in the car she just hit. "What the hell are you doing stopping in the middle of America's busiest freeway? Look, look, five-fucking-car pile-up."

Jumble painfully opened her eyes. They felt glued shut. She made a mental note never to get her eyebrows waxed. She turned to get out of her car but her shoulder wouldn't move. She looked out the window, and she saw a woman with little rings of white around her nose. Jumble started to laugh. Her clavicle was probably broken. She more than likely was concussed, and she had this beautiful teeth-baring, eyebrow-scrunching, arm-waving, white-ringed-nose woman screaming at her. It reminded her of an episode of *I Love Lucy* or maybe it was *Laverne and Shirley*. She did kind of feel as if her synapse was misfiring. "Powder," someone would call and a big puff of powder would hit the comedienne's face. This woman standing outside Jumble's car looked like a small termite had powdered her face. The other thing Jumble felt was relief. It was the first time in years she felt like she was in real time. All those days, all those hours that she felt her time was eating up her life had for a brief minute slowed into that watch-the-clock impatience. Later, Jey's attorney pleaded down the driving under the influence charge, as long as Jey went to A.A. meetings and stayed sober for sixty days.

"You know I hate to tell you this," Jey confessed to Jumble. "Sometimes I'm at a meeting and I've had a few beers. You know I'm drunk and I'm sitting there listening to everybody and I know I'm not like them. My cousin Ronnie is like them, and my next door neighbor is like them but I'm not like them. I'm an atheist. I can't surrender to a higher nonexistent power." Jumble didn't know what to think. Jey was her higher nonexistent power.

The next time Jey wasn't as lucky. She had been giving her soliloquy at the Kangaroo Coffee House. Her head twisted for nearly thirty minutes, screaming. "Half eaten yogurt, half an order of eggs Benedict, half a tuna sandwich, half moon harvest, half and half make a whole but only this once or is it twice? Half a twin sister, half an orange, half an X chromosome makes a Y or is it? Half of your fucking heart. Half of your asexual, amoral fallopian tube. You were inside her. You penetrated her. Half a million. What do I have to do for it? Can you hear me? No, can you hear me? Did someone fix the short in the mike jack? What do I have to do? I'm going to electrocute myself."

As she continued, Jey swung the jar with the scalp inside of it in a semicircle, then she would stop and swing it the other way. To most, even Jumble, the object inside the jar looked like a hairpiece floating in water. They would watch it, transfixed, as it sloshed slowly from one end of the jar to the other.

"What? On my knees? On my back? On my ass? Up my . . . " As she said it, the jar flew from her hand and hit a man in the back while he was having a vanilla latte with skim milk. If it had been anyone else, the assailant would have quickly run over to the man and asked if he was all right. Jey was not that charming and she was in the middle of one of her greatest moments. The Ginsberg Soliloquy.

"What?" Jey asked. "Seeing my generation. Well, fuck off. My generation is blank. Do you understand? My generation is what every other generation has sucked dry. We are the empty bone and we still must produce the marrow. I've seen the greatest minds of . . . my generation can't see. What? We can't love. We can't fuck. We can't die and we have no right to." Jey screamed. "You don't like me. You don't like me? I don't care. Can you hear me? Fucking mike."

Jumble watched the man get up and stagger to Jey. He was a medium-built man. He looked like a medium intelligent man. He had an oblong chin and that might have been the only thing not medium about him. The man grabbed Jey and slurred his anger over her face. "Say it. Say you're sorry. I didn't come here to see you. I came to see Tricky Dick the Magician. I don't like your stupid poetry. I don't like your bellyaches. How old are you? Well, I was in the Gulf War. I'm a killer."

Jey grabbed the mike and tore off the cord and shoved it into the man's mouth. He fell to his knees, shaking and shuddering from the electricity.

"The very best minds of my generation electrocuted," Jey screamed.

This time Jey wasn't so lucky. She was charged with assault and battery, and went to jail. The LAPD confiscated the scalp and put it into evidence. The jar didn't break when it hit the man, so the LAPD didn't investigate the floating hairpiece. They figured it was a wig stored in water. Jey received eighteen months and the issue about Jackson's disappearance never came up. Most believe she got away with murder.

Jumble walked into the room, escorted by the prison guard. She could see Jey through the glass and she sat in the chair in front of Jey. It was one of those moments when she wished she had a camera. Jumble watched Jey pick up the phone. Jumble's lips were dry.

"Ginsberg. He's dead." Jumble moistened the words over her lips.

Jey put down the phone and for the first time silently howled for her generation.

Tavia Ervin

◆

The Pastor's Wife

Sunday there was tuna fish salad and the Old Testament. Susannah always thought that when she was very old and losing her senses that she would remember those two things every Sunday. Today there had been lettuce and tomato, pickles, potato salad and canned peaches also. The table was strewn with bread crumbs and dirty dishes. The relish dish was sticky with the remains of the sweet gherkins. The ice had melted in the tea glasses, but the three women still sat at the table. Eunice sat in the chair nearest to the kitchen. From this chair she was always the first to jump up for whatever anyone needed. Alma, the older sister, sat with her cat in her lap. She patted the animal's head and little wisps of white fur flew through the air. The cat was enormous, with a big drooping belly and large gold-green eyes. Alma looked like a child as she stroked the cat and spoke softly to her. Eunice disapproved of animals at the table and rolled her eyes at her granddaughter who sat across from her. Broad rays of sun came in through the open windows to hypnotize the women. The day was getting hotter, but every once in a while a faint breeze touched them.

Susannah thought back on the morning. The dark sanctuary full of old people, the cool smooth pews that smelled of tung oil. It had always been the same there, for as long as she could remember. Old men in their one suit for the season and the women in their best print dresses. The pastor distant and benevolent in his black single-breasted suit — always the same. Everything that was fine and decent about their lives was captured in that church, but it really had very little to do with God. Their attempts to be good citizens, fathers, mothers, PTA presidents, neighborhood boosters — that was what lingered there and even though it had very little in it of spiritual passion, it was comforting and safe in the church. Susannah had never seen an emotional outburst there or heard an inspired confession. Most of them were coming to the ends of their lives and in their minds that fact somehow eliminated the need for confession.

"Eunice, that sunshine will fade your carpeting," Alma said. "I was careful about that when I was in my own house." She had lived with her sister for years, ever since her husband died. Eunice didn't care about things like faded rugs, but she couldn't resist a comment.

"I'm not worried about it. The layer of cat hair should keep it from fading."

"You're mean, Eunice," said Alma, but she said it matter-of-factly without anger or hurt in her voice. "She's always been kind of mean." This time she spoke to Susannah.

"Come on. Don't start this," said Eunice impatiently. "Let's take our tea outside and sit in the backyard." Susannah got up to clear the table.

"Don't touch a dish," said her grandmother. "We'll get them later. Let's spend all our time visiting."

Susannah picked up her iced tea glass and reached for her grandmother's. "Want a refill?"

"I think I've had enough. I feel like an old ship taking on water."

"How about you, Aunt Alma?"

"No dear, I'm fine."

Susannah pushed her chair back to rise and refill her glass, when she stopped at the sound of sobbing. She sat back down and peered through the screen into the yard next door. Because the houses were so close together, it took no effort at all to see what the neighbors were doing in their backyards or who drove into their driveways for a visit. Eunice saw this as an advantage since most of the women on her block were widows living alone or in pairs. She always said there was a comfort for her in knowing that her routines were well known by all, so that anything unusual would alert her neighbors to a problem. Several times the city police had been called to their street because a strange car was in a driveway or a new face was seen coming and going.

Over on Doris Fink's back stoop sat Mrs. Brecht, crying. She wasn't crying silently, but in great gulping sobs. She patted herself softly on the chest with her fist.

"Is that Reverend Brecht's wife?" asked Susannah.

"Yes, that's her. I don't know what she's doing over at Doris'. She's been crazy lately, I heard from Clara Peterson." Alma leaned forward slightly to see better. "She's always been so standoffish, hasn't she Eunice? Your kids and hers went all through school together and she has never been all that friendly, has she?"

Eunice didn't say anything, just looked hard at Mrs. Brecht for a while. "She's always kept to herself, but I don't know what's wrong now. This isn't like her."

"Someone needs to help her," said Susannah, setting her glass down. She got up to go to the woman.

"Don't go over there!" Her grandmother touched her arm. "There's not a thing you can do for her. Some of the women at the church have tried to help her, but she just insists that people are against her. She doesn't even trust her poor old husband."

"We can't just ignore her over there." The touch to her arm had caused Susannah to pause. She looked down at her grandmother, who was looking over at the woman again.

"It's the pastor I feel sorry for," Alma said. "To be prominent in the community like that all these years and then have her go like this." Alma made a spinning gesture at her temple to indicate Rose Brecht's mental state.

"I can't just watch this go on without saying something to her." Susannah walked out the back door to the gate in the fence, unlatched it and crossed into the next yard. As she went over to where the woman was sitting, she had no idea what she was going to say to her.

Rose looked up. "Hello honey," she said. "I'm just waiting here for Doris to get home. I thought maybe I could visit with some of the neighbors."

Susannah stood there silently.

Rose Brecht was a big woman who had always worn her hair tightly in a neat bun at the base of her neck. Today her hair was pulled back loosely into a low ponytail. She was dressed all in white. White work pants — the kind that painters wear on the job. A man's white T-shirt.

Susannah's voice sounded more distressed than the older woman's. "What's wrong, Mrs. Brecht?" Susannah sat down on the cool concrete steps next to her.

"I have no one." The older woman stated it flatly as if it were the most objective, obvious thing she could have said. She stopped crying, but her face was still grim. "My husband thinks I'm crazy. After all this time. I did so much for him — so many years — and now I'm alone. Without my children, too." At the mention of her children, suddenly she looked like a model pastor's wife — very upright and proper. Susannah felt foolish at witnessing the woman's personal moment.

"I raised six of them, you know. Four and a set of twins, and now I don't have them either." With that she pulled up the front of her shirt. The motion of her arms was so quick compared to her other movements that Susannah thought for a moment that she was going to hit her. When she lifted the shirt, Susannah could see parts of her white skin, laced with blue veins. The skin of the old that looked so vulnerable and embarrassed. Across her stomach she had tied a carpenter's white cotton nail apron.

"Let me show you a picture," she said, and began flipping through a bundle of papers she had in the apron. "I have my insurance policy here. I take it with me wherever I go now." She fumbled through other papers and finally came up with the photograph. It was a family snapshot with all of her children and grandchildren grouped around her and her husband, the pastor.

"What a nice-looking family," Susannah said, and immediately felt self-conscious. The words were something that her grandmother or aunt or any of the older women might say. They felt strange and somehow disrespectful coming out of her mouth, like the understudy speaking the lines of the lead. She asked for the names of the children and grandchildren in the picture.

Rose patted her on the hand and smiled. "Old pictures of strangers are so sad somehow, don't you think?"

She sighed and Susannah sat silently looking at the photograph. "Oh God, please let me know what to say," she prayed silently to herself, but no inspiration came. All around them the day continued on. The sun shone, cars went up and down the street out front, fat robins poked around on the ground for food, and the pastor's wife was losing her mind. Susannah looked up and down the backyards that stretched on forever in both directions. How many other people were losing their minds today?

She took Rose's hand. "Do you want to come over and sit with us?"

"No, no. I'll just sit here and wait. Doris should be home soon." She fumbled again with the papers in the nail apron. Susannah looked over at the house and could see her grandmother and aunt through the window. Aunt Alma motioned frantically for her to come back. Susannah ignored her and turned her head.

"Yes, I've got my insurance policy." She produced a crumpled white paper certificate edged with green filigree designs. Susannah took the insurance policy and pretended to look it over while she tried to decide what to do. As she looked at the paper, Rose talked on and on about the contents of the nail pouch. "Here's some of my own money." She pulled out a small roll of bills held together with a rubber band. "And I have some Kennedy half-dollars that I collect — they're very heavy." She laid the roll of money and a dozen half dollars on the space of concrete between them. "I also have my bank book with his name on it, too. He doesn't even know it's gone. Maybe he'll think one of the children took it."

Rose grinned at Susannah cheerfully now and Susannah patted her arm. "Everything will be all right. Please let me call someone for you so you can go home."

Immediately Mrs. Brecht's bottom lip began to quiver again and the space between her eyebrows scrunched together in a row of wrinkles. "You know, dear, that before you have a baby you'll have to toughen up your breasts to feed it."

The unexpected subject took Susannah by surprise and she didn't answer.

Mrs. Brecht didn't know the difference and went on. "I used a toothbrush on mine until they bled because I wanted to do it just right. I was so young." She turned a little from Susannah and began to cry to herself.

Susannah felt irritated and panicked. Now that she was here, what should she do? She thought that Mrs. Brecht would be happy just for the company and attention and would agree to go home once she got a little of both. What did she want? She heard the rusty gate in the fence open and close and looked up to see her grandmother coming toward them. She looked beyond her grandmother at the window where Aunt Alma sat framed like a nineteenth century portrait, with folded arms and disapproving frown.

"Oh Eunice, I thought you might come over. Susannah and I were having a visit." Mrs. Brecht patted the step on her left. "Come join us."

"Rose, what's the problem?" her grandmother asked very sternly.

Mrs. Brecht smiled up at her with tears running down her face. "Oh, it's nothing really, Eunice. Susannah here is so nice to have come over and to check up on me, though. And you too. I appreciate it."

"You really ought to go on home now. Come on over to my house and I'll call your husband for you."

"I'll just wait for Doris," she said firmly. "You know she's cut my hair for years, now." She patted her head absently. The tears flowed again.

It was Eunice's turn to be frustrated. "You mean you're over here waiting for a haircut? It's Sunday, Rose. Doris is visiting her mother."

Rose's expression did not change. "I don't need a haircut," she said. "I'm just waiting here for her. I've known her for a long time." She looked away from Susannah and Eunice as she spoke.

Eunice sighed and sat down on the step below Rose and Susannah, facing them. "What's going on, Rose?" She spoke more tenderly this time.

"Are you ever lonely, Eunice?" she asked. "Do you ever wish for someone to say anything you please to?" Rose cried as she spoke and Susannah and her grandmother sat quietly listening to her and to the summer noises of the neighborhood — lawnmowers and dogs and children playing.

"Come back in, Eunice. You too, Susie. Come in now and leave her be." At first it was not clear where the voice had come from, but there was Alma sitting in the window speaking through thin tight lips. They ignored her.

Suddenly Donna Keller appeared in front of them and leaned over the fence. "Is Doris home?"

Mrs. Brecht didn't pay any attention to the question and Susannah suddenly realized how strange it must look for all of them to be sitting in someone's backyard when that someone wasn't even home. Eunice gestured toward the pastor's wife. "Rose is waiting for her and we're just keeping her company."

"Come and sit down with us." The pastor's wife was quick with the invitation. Donna nodded her little bottle-blonde head and came through the gate with crisp efficient steps.

"Aren't you feeling well?" she shouted at Rose while she looked at Eunice. Susannah was embarrassed on Rose's behalf, but she didn't seem to notice the tone or the implication of the question.

"Do you have anyone, Donna?" Rose said, looking up bleary-eyed with crying.

"I've got my husband . . . " Donna's voice trailed off and she was obviously confused by a question that she thought everyone in the neighborhood should know the answer to.

"You don't have to wait here with us, Donna," Eunice said hopefully. "Doris won't be back for quite a while so we're just talking to Rose while she waits."

"That's fine with me," said Donna, pulling up a lawn chair. "It's so cool and restful in this yard. I'll just sit for a while, too. Where's Alma? Oh, there she is. Hello, Alma. Come join us." Donna waved energetically. Alma nodded her head slightly but otherwise didn't move. Donna settled in, ignoring Rose's crying. "I'm getting ready to have my carpets professionally shampooed," she began. "As soon as they're done, we're going to a resort in the Ozarks for two weeks. The place is called Cedar Crest Cove and they supply everything but the bed linen, which I'd rather supply myself because you just can't expect people to take the same care with laundering whites as you do yourself."

Susannah watched some ants transport bread crumbs across the cement sidewalk. Mrs. Brecht sat crying and Eunice stared straight ahead, thinking, her hands on her knees.

"Here comes old Lettie Griggs out in the hot of the day in her sweater. That damned white sweater." Aunt Alma spoke like a Greek chorus. Susannah looked up. Mrs. Griggs was making her way toward them across the yards in a red dress. Through each gate, turning to latch the gate behind her, walking across the yard, unlatching the gate, walking through, turning to latch the gate behind her. Rhythmic, like the steps of a grand dance slowed down in a dream — through, back, forward, stop, through, back, forward, stop — the same number of steps in each yard, a census of the neighborhood as she came toward them. She was old, old, old and wore a sweater across her shoulders twelve months of the year. As Aunt Alma had announced, she wore one today — an immaculately white sweater positioned perfectly. She finally reached the women and pulled up a chair without saying anything.

"It's good to see you, Lettie," said Mrs. Brecht. "Do you have anyone to talk to?"

Susannah winced at the question and was glad that Lettie, who had been widowed for thirty years, could hardly hear. Donna kept up her steady stream of chatter without pause. "Does anyone ever really hear?" Rose spoke to herself as much as to anyone else.

They sat there for a while, silent except for Donna. Lettie Griggs nodded off a bit and a breeze blew over them gently.

"Come back over here, you two. I'm all by myself. Good Lord, this whole thing is just silly." Alma spoke again just as the gate at the back of the yard clanked and Lil Schultz struggled into the yard pulling grandchildren from her legs like little burrs. She was younger than the other women — about fifty — and always had grandchildren with her.

"Is this a party?" she asked, and sat down without an invitation or another comment, except to tell the children who had followed her to "go find Grandpa." They ran back through the gate and across the alley to her yard.

"Wouldn't some cool melon be good?" Eunice asked.

"The melon has been good and sweet this year," Donna agreed.

Rose sniffed and watched a big loud jay chase a starling from its nest. Without taking her eyes off the birds, she spoke to the women. "Everyone expects melon in the summer, don't they? But I hate it. There you are, cutting it and serving it at every picnic and church social and neighborhood cookout you go to — giving everybody what they expect. It's too sticky and sweet and yet there's really nothing to it, is there? It's all just water, though it seems like more."

"We've had some great summers together in this neighborhood, haven't we?" Eunice said.

"Too much melon." Rose stated it as a matter of known fact.

"What in the hell are you going on about, Rose?" asked Lil. "You've got a lot more to worry about than how much watermelon everybody's eaten over the last forty years. When is Nathan coming to get you?"

"I'm not waiting for Nathan," Mrs. Brecht said. "I'm here to see Doris and as many of the neighbors as I can. We've been talking about being alone."

"Alone? That's rich. I wish I could have some time alone. I just got done raising my own and now they bring all theirs over. Why would I want to talk about being alone?" Lil broke off short and looked at the ground for a moment before she changed the subject. "Doris is at her mother's and might not be back till late. Maybe not at all. Sometimes she spends the night."

The pastor's wife was not interested. "Pick one of those children and really talk to them. Maybe you'll have one person in the end who hears you."

Lil rolled her eyes and shook her head in a combination of disbelief and disapproval.

"I can go get my cookies." Lettie Griggs had awakened suddenly and rose stiffly. "I'll be right back." She left the yard and Donna waved at Alma again. She did not wave back.

"You all really don't have to wait here," Susannah said. The silence between them made her uncomfortable and she felt somehow responsible for filling it. She was annoyed with that feeling. Rose said nothing, but cried again silently.

"You could go home." Eunice looked off in the direction of Lil's house, apparently hoping she'd remember some unmet grandchild's need and rush off.

Instead she sat forward with her knees apart and reached into her pocket for a leatherette cigarette case. "I'm pretty comfortable. Don can chase the kids around for a while." She stretched out her legs in front of her and took out a cigarette. "Do any of you mind?" she said, waving her cigarette in their general direction and lighting a match. Lil pointed to Rose. "This could be any of us in a few years." She took a long drag on her cigarette. No one said a word.

"You should just go home," Aunt Alma said.

"What?" Lil looked up to see Alma in her window. "Well, hey Alma, I didn't see you over there. Come on out here and join the party."

"You should go home, Lil." Alma's voice was even and calm. Lil rolled her eyes and gestured with her head in Alma's direction. The others ignored her. They could hear her grandchildren squabbling over a game in their yard across the alley. Lil ignored them. The women looked away from each other, except for Rose, who silently gazed at their faces with watery, swollen eyes.

The afternoon passed. Lettie Griggs returned with some lemon sugar cookies on a gold-rimmed plate decorated with violets. "We could sing a hymn," she said after a while and she hummed "Blest Be the Tie That Binds."

No one joined her.

Donna told Lil about her brother-in-law's success at giving up cigarettes. "He swears he could not taste food anymore, he'd smoked for so long. Now it's like he's got a new life or something. Food tastes better and his clothes don't stink." Lil looked amused through a cloud of blue smoke.

Eunice spoke quietly to Rose. "How are you feeling now, Rose?"

The pastor's wife looked at her and took her hand. "Don't ask me that Eunice, because you don't really want to know. I know that because I've never cared what happened to any of you. While Nathan spent all his time counseling you and christening your babies and preaching to you about the kingdom of heaven, I could have cared less about any of you. You don't want to know how I feel because it's too painful and you've got enough of your own, I guess."

They all paid attention that time. Lettie Griggs looked like she might start crying. Donna's little flat face was blank and Lil hung her head and ground out her cigarette into the sidewalk. Susannah put her hand on her grandmother's shoulder. Her grandma held Rose's hand. On and on the afternoon went and the talk was the same. Early evening came on. Cicadas began their mating song and lawnmowers were parked in garages. Families settled down for their Sunday-evening-before-Monday-morning ritual.

Alma left the window and came back with a cheese sandwich. "I don't feel so sorry for the pastor anymore. Now come back in."

Martha McGill

Poems

On Writing

one

the wordspring flows
when tidewater pulls
at the deep and quiet
silt of dreams
sharp fresh current
stirs sleeping thoughts
for a time infuses them
with life

    two

    poems are born
    in expectation
    words are the building blocks
    the way up and out

        three

        playing with words
        from the storehouse
        where i live
        inside the one
        others think i am
        what a game of hide and seek
        a writer plays

Old Photographs: 1860-1900

I have a package
In the attic
Old, old prints
Mounted on heavy cards
As though the man
Who made them knew
I'd need them now

All my people . . .
Stiffly posed, unsmiling
Clothes not for comfort
But for funerals
Weddings
And for cameras

Behind their eyes I see
Land cleared and furrowed
Houses raised cows milked
Eggs gathered
Babies born and buried
Wagons packed and drawn
Out of Virginia through the Gap
Into river country
South of the Ohio — East of the Father
Of Waters
Helping displace the sons of sons
Of moundbuilders

The prints are dusty like their lives
Earth clung to them
They did not live apart as I have

I'd sweep earth floors
Dig water wells
Plant summer's table in the spring
If I could reach beyond flat images

Into my family

Blow me a shape

Blow me a shape
Then send me soaring
Chord me with earthsong
Resonant, deep

Temper with breezes
Through crystalline branches
Use hills for sounding
Wake me from sleep

from its waters we all rise

from its waters we all rise
nourished by the silt of dreams
find our air
sprout our limbs
open wings
complicate our thinking-parts
with paths unnumbered
set the whorls
in elegant connecting webs
activate ten thousand years
of parentage unchosen
announce our
selves
create a person
tapestried with multi-colors
strand by strand
sculpt ourselves
from living rock
weather storms
and learn that gales
are not to crumble
but refine

We were summer's children

We were summer's children
Making ropes of clover
Reach across the road, and more
Splitting dandelion stems
To change, with chilly water
In Shirley Temple curls
Holding blades of grass
In folded hands, against small lips
Blowing piercing whistles
At the sky

Grandma's bed at naptime
Full of us, and bubbling laughter
As we tried not to look
Into each other's eyes

Hiding counting seeking
Under summer's-evening trees
Oldest telling ghostly tales
Enjoying younger shrieks
In dark front yards

Making songs inside, with nonsense words
Like combuloosy, nonfonsay
And others unremembered
Pulling chains on cuckoo clocks
To still the passing time
Or make the bird come out

Summers never seemed to end
In my heart we all stay young
Forever

and here i am

the body: large and sluggish
its age becoming evident
its slender youth a memory
healed of some faults
with others lying dormant waiting
    for their turn
strength not yet lost but waning
    a host . . . abiding
through its time of consciousness
existing as a vehicle
    in a brief passage

    with companions

    to an undiscovered destiny

and here "I" too
the spirit: not resting in the flesh
    intangible . . . illimitable
        no mass to measure

        I cannot be described

        in mortal terms

    my source unguessed
    my final home a mystery

the wanderer, twisting through,
    pathfinder on a journey
    made by one
        alone

Look at me

Look at me
With your cheetah eyes
As I stand in clarity
Against a blurred landscape
Prey to your skill

All she could do was look at us

All she could do was look at us
in silence at the end
There is no salve to soothe this surgery
of her life from ours
No techniques of transplantation
could restore our clasped hands
her voice that carried
messages beyond the words
We are diminished by her element
air water fire are less
since she is now subtracted
from the sum of us
I miss her burning eyes

Across the pasture

Across the pasture
of my father's failing farm
I sensed a wolf.
It threatened and enticed
my life, barring me
from the elegance of the only
water-spring I ever knew.
I still desire the touch,
the sight of clean sand
welling into swirling crystal
in that sun-baked, thirsty place.

outrageous!!

Aristotle called the sex
that gave him birth
deficient males
                            [philosophy distorted]

Milton called us
a pretty mistake
                            [shame on you poet]

Nietzche said
when you go to a woman
don't forget your whip
                            [amoral nazi before hitler]

Schopenhauer called women
childish frivolous immature
big children monkey-like
                            [is this deep thought]

Victor Hugo quoted
God made himself man
the devil made himself woman
                            [disappointing and he also
                              wrote *Les Miserables*]

Dumas propounded
according to the Bible
woman was the last thing God
created   obviously it was on
Saturday night when he was
very tired
                            [unfunny]

OUTRAGE = RAPE
RAPE = ATROCITY

Martha McGill

◆

Hairpeace

When I was a youngster, my trips to the barbershop were too frequent for my taste! I had to first endure the dread of the event for several days. On the fateful day, the walk to the shop seemed "the last mile" of my childish reluctance to be shorn of my only attractive feature, as I perceived my looks at the time.

Since no appointments were ever made for the cutting ritual, only when entering the shop would I learn whether my terror would be prolonged for any amount of time, for other customers — always male! always old! — or be cut blessedly to a short visit (almost private) because no one else was waiting. There was comfort in the latter: the barber would not feel compelled to make any loud jokes for his usual audience of people like himself. There would be no pressure to put me quickly through my torture, so the group could resume their "barbershop humor" sessions after my departure. I would be treated like a child, not like a miniature adult who somehow was expected to respond to remarks made by the barber or his compatriots who often found it amusing to say things not really aimed at me, but which obviously called for some comment from the occupant of the chair. My inability to make immediate sharp, clever returns to their overtures was a source of somewhat twisted pleasure to those gentlemen, whose attitude toward children while not in the barbershop was acceptable and caused no damage. I never personally verified the stories one heard about publications of questionable moral value being available in barbershops, but there did seem to be an atmosphere there of release from normal rules of behavior, and my presence did nothing to alter that.

My haircuts were always the same: bangs cut straight across my forehead just above my eyebrows, the tops of my ears allowed to show just below the so-called "Dutch bob" of my side hair, and worst of all, "shingled" in the back! This made me look at once like a combination of at least three cultures — English, maybe Dutch (though I was never blonde) and possibly Scottish (the shingle part, which didn't require cutting as often).

Most of my schoolmates, neighbors and cousins did not have to endure the same kind of barbershop visits but were allowed to have long hair, and sometimes even use a curling iron upon which the hair was rolled and tied into place until the linseed oil setting lotion (homemade) had created waves and curls. Some had braided hair, which looked wavy when the braids were loosened. My style was a 1920s one, which my mother found to be attractive on herself, but this was now the thirties and more glamorous looks were coming. No amount of wheedling on my part would change the decision to make me into a copy of my mother's generation.

Toward the end of that decade, when we moved to Illinois from Kentucky, the women and girls were so different in appearance from my mother and me that she began to allow her hair to grow and be curled in the fashion of the times. By the advent of the forties, I also was excused from the aberration of always being out of step with my peers. I recall the extreme relief I felt when I could finally put a barrette in my former bangs and pull my hair to the side! When I was seventeen, my hair still remained uncut and I reveled in the freedom of it! In the fifties, I pulled my hair back in a ponytail or a chignon, which set off my long streak (naturally grey, since age 11), and never felt the cold steel of scissors. Everything stayed that way, until I was out of fashion and felt compelled to have it styled to the shortest length I could stand. The hairdresser who performed the deed shed real tears, bemoaning the loss of my lovely dark brown waist-length tresses — that is, until I told her to sell the cuttings for her own profit. It gave me pleasure to know that someone who needed hair would receive mine.

Somehow this saga of how my hair and my sense of worth were "of a piece" revealed to me the importance of being fair with my own daughter and sons, who have always chosen their own styles with my blessings.

Becky Bradway

◆

From *Searching for the Muses*

Melissa, 35, is a musician and elementary school teacher whose personal life and visions bring her into conflict with her family and her political ideas, and cause social gossip and other troublesome situations. Kimmy is her partner in their folk-punk band, The Muses.

Kimmy's apartment is in a complex. She calls it the oedipal complex, though it's really the electra complex. This is the first time I've seen it with all the furniture; after getting out of rehab, she stayed with her mom for a while, and she's only been settled here a week. It isn't anything like the sort of place she usually chooses. This is so clean and new it seems like a social conversion.

The binge she went on before committing herself to treatment was the postpartum of being dumped by her favorite lover. But Ramon took pity and now they're back together, except he lives in Chicago. "Long distance," Kimmy likes to tell people, "makes us glad to be together." It also allows them to take on other lovers the way some people collect Precious Moments dolls. Kimmy keeps condoms in her purse in the same type of zippered compartment where I keep a tiny notebook and pen. So it's a shiny new life with the same old iron bed.

"This place looks like it was designed for bachelorette number two," I notice as we walk up the white metal staircase.

"I see it more as a Holiday Inn just for me." Kimmy works her key into the door. I look over the railing at the swimming pool where a shirtless man sits reading at poolside.

"It's fifty degrees and he's getting a tan."

"No, he's just showing off his abs to the babes. His face, though, looks like Walter Brennan."

"At least it's not Ned Beatty." We stumble into darkness; Kimmy switches on the antique lamp. I set my guitar against the wicker couch and hang my suede jacket in a closet already stuffed with coats, shawls, snazzy sweaters. "This place looks like Casablanca," I say, looking at the ceiling fan. "All you need is a parrot."

"I'm thinking of getting a crow; want a beer?"

"Sure." I'll nurse it most of the evening. I follow her into what can only be called a kitchenette and sit at the formica-topped counter. The appliances are miniature, almond-colored, made for people so on the go that they never need to cook for themselves or anyone else. "I don't think I've had a new stove in my life. Does it clean itself?"

She twists the cap off a Molson's and hands it to me. "Are you making fun of my pad?" I wasn't, but it's nice that she doesn't just consider me a domestic mom-type. We talk about moving in, sorting boxes — all the details of transience and temporary settlement — when she says, with this glint in her eye, "Guess what I got."

She heads off to her entertainment center (shelving pre-installed) in the living room and comes back with a CD. From the picture — man w/guitar a la Dylan, wimpy grin — I know even before she presses it into my hand.

"Sherman." I want to laugh; I want to cry; but mostly I'm irritated that I have to deal with it. I thought this was personal; yet here's my life, in multiple copies and sold in the folk bin at Best Buy.

"I thought it would be fun to pick apart all the songs that are about you."

"Yeah. Loads." I keep a tight hold on the box so Kimmy can't grab it back and harass me with it. I have friends all over the state whose favorite game is figuring out which songs are about me — people who know the music scene, who think it's a hoot. For me, it was the spark that blew up my marriage, and the one that made a mess of his; for them, it's just whispers and fascination. Voyeuristic sport.

Not that I hold it against Kimmy. I find it puzzlelike to pick apart the songs, too. For a long time, I was flattered, the way a muse ought to be. But as it dragged on over one CD and another, with pieces of my body and my life popping up like cutouts from magazines and formed into Sherman's own collage, beyond my control, and I came to understand that he was never going to actually come into my life, I started feeling, well . . . "Look, he's just using me. Every poet is a thief."

"Oh, but it's awfully pretty music. I think I'd get off on someone writing songs about me."

"I guess I do. I sort of do." Especially at first. Each one a surprising, strange flower, set to wilt or burst in my hands. I loved them, played them over and over, in an awe that he could make of it all something truly perfect. My mistake was in thinking they could exist outside of their own sphere; that they could be planted in the yards of my world. Now I have the CD's, but have only played this new one a few times, just to know what he's up to, what he has to say. "It's not like he's really in my life."

"Maybe he just likes to play. So tell me." Kimmy leans on the counter, so close to my face I can smell the peppers from our Thai supper. Her round yin-yang necklace has settled into the hollow of her neck. "What do they mean? They're so artistic. So packed full of metaphors. One thing meaning another."

"Yeah. Those are secrets." I look glumly at the photo. He's got that sensitive poetic look. This from a guy who on a drunken night screamed at random strangers on the street just because he felt like it. Who sat in the limbs of a tree singing Beatles songs, passing down this bottle of Jim Beam to me on the limb below, until the cops kicked us out of the park. All that wildness of art that had a lot more to do with grabbing the clouds than with pained reflection. As it should be. I stuff the CD under my armpit.

"The song about birds — that's really you, right? Birds to fly out of his poor trapped little yard; I feel so sorry for the guy."

"Oh, come on, Kimmy. He's perfectly happy where he is. If he wasn't, he'd leave." Birds equal flight equal transcendence equal leaving tough marriage equal ethereal and sexless love for her. Or me, I guess, if she is me. Or whatever he's made of me, which is a distantly safe unreal image who never talks back. An image he can say is all made up, a construction of his imagination. Sure, and I could point out that in the song it refers to the pizza we ate four years ago and the guy in the corner of the restaurant who picked up a guitar and played "Stairway to Heaven" oh so badly and oh so romantically, and that there are snippets of our conversation that night, repeated verbatim but only I would know that so how can I prove it and should I and to whom? Explaining the song would mean explaining why the night and the words had mattered and even in repeating the words it would diminish the event which is already disappearing it having been four years ago as I try so hard to avoid him yet the songs just keep fuckin coming like the hits and Kimmy'd just only half believe me anyway and so why try?

"I don't know what it means," I lie. Actually, the song is quite clear. But you kinda had to be there.

"Oh! You're so frustrating!" Her hair flops into her face and her fishnet sleeves slide down her elbows so she can still show off her bracelets. They dangle when she makes a grab for the CD.

I sit on it — the only time I'll even come close to sitting on Sherman's face, too bad for him.

She yells, "I want to hear the good stuff! I love obsession!"

"It's overrated. Listen, Kimmy, the guy is bored. First he loves me, then he hates me, he thinks I'm an angel, he thinks I'm a slut, he can't have me, he doesn't want me, and it's melodrama is what it's about and that's all there is to it." But that doesn't keep it from crying when I play the CD, which is only in my saddest or sweetest moods; doesn't keep the songs from coming into my head at the strangest times, like when I'm driving or half asleep; doesn't keep me from wishing sometimes that it could be, even when the thought that it actually could be terrifies me. I never met anyone so much like me before, I want to say to Kimmy. Someone who thinks in symbols and signs and signals and allusions; yet this is just what keeps it shifty and secretive. Keeps it as much of a song of cheating lies as any in a Hank Williams collection. Because if I get it, and hardly anyone else, then his ass is covered and his wife is deceived. And is it good to know somebody just like me? Or is there danger in that blending of ideas, images, rage, joy, hair/face/style/attitude/background — maybe we're not meant to know our twin, our other.

"If I met this guy," Kimmy says, pulling a hunk of her purple hair through her fingers, "I could psych him out for you. Maybe we can get him here. He's kind of cute, in a kidlike nerdy sort of way."

"I don't want to see him," I say, this both a lie and the truth. "But, yeah, he's pretty sweet." Because I met him at music festivals and poetry workshops, nobody around here knows him. This adds to the disconnected, out-of-time, super-romanticized, downright weird feel. For a while, I wanted him in my world. I wanted it real. I wanted to spend my life with him, making breakfasts and mowing lawns like editing words. I believed him.

"He'd just charm you," I say.

"What about that song about being a miner and digging through the past? That has to be you."

"Naw. I don't know what he's talking about."

That lovely song, maybe my favorite, is about when I looked into the pit of my life. All these things I had talked to him about one long night over beer. All of it in the song, right down to the Van Morrison lyric we sang, leaning against the wall beneath the baseball pennants. There are people who look at me as if I made him write that song. But I just told the story. I didn't even touch him for emphasis.

"You're no fun," Kimmy says.

Sure, I tried to get him to come to me. After my divorce. I thought he wanted to. I thought that's what the songs were: signals. Callings. Messages. I thought he was telling me he was coming. That spring would come and there he would be. Like the song said.

After a while, I let it go. I like being alone. I really do. So I was gullible. Big dumb me. "It's all a hunka burning romantic crud," I say. "That's what life's about, right?"

But for Kimmy, sex and romance are one and the same and about as casual as her daily jog. "Why not go for it? This celibacy thing of yours is all screwed up. Just sleep with him. Sleep with Daniel, too; you know he wants to. I've seen that look in his eye when he sees you. Why do you have to be so prim?"

I have to laugh. "Everyone thinks I do it anyway," though I don't have any intention of going for it. Not without some certainty of future. I wrote Sherman a sexy letter once; but he'll never act. It's safe for me, too.

"You're afraid to take risks, so you stick yourself with these obsessive loser guys who make phone calls and then don't talk."

"I never should have mentioned that to you."

"You ought to be getting yourself laid. Three years is too long."

"It's not quite three years." It's really two and a half. "Hey, I can't even handle my fantasies. I don't know what I'd do with real life."

"Real life is easier." Kimmy slides off the stool and goes to her cabinets, starts rooting. Her green midi-shirt pulls up, showing the edge of her violet bra.

"Like hell. I've had real life. I know what it's like." I look at Sherman's CD face, smiling benignly unless you look closely; then you see it, that hint of smugness, of anger, that working class kid getting over by any means look that I know because I have it, too. Determination against numerous boots in the face. It makes you kind of a jerk. It makes everyone fair game. My angel-wing flutter of excitement is gone. Now I get that with Daniel. Looking at Sherman, I just feel this loss. Like maybe it might have been, or had been in some other life, in some way I can't grasp and can never understand.

"Well, screw it. I give up." She tosses a bag of mini-Reese's peanut butter cups on the counter, goes in the other room, comes back with my guitar. "Punky's next Saturday! Whatcha got new?"

"Just one." I dig in my pocket for this sheet I wrote up yesterday, all folded into a square. I think of this game I used to play in junior high, a paper creased into triangles with a message under each flap. This is what lyric is for me: always a secret, always a surprise. "And I know everyone will think it's about Sherman. But I'm not sure who it's about. Maybe it's about me."

Kimmy wanders into the bedroom, right off the kitchenette, and yells out, "I have a dress with silver spangles just for this show. Got it at Ali's Thrift. I'm going to wear a tiara! With my silver heels, the clunky ones with the ankle strap."

Guess I'll go look. Kimmy likes folks to look. But I don't. I put Sherman back on her CD shelf, mixing it in with the others, out of order. I'll just wear jeans on the stage. I don't like everyone staring at me. That way, I can watch.

Sue Sitki

◆

Undernight

San Francisco. Mission district. "The Elbow Room."
 The bartender smiled as he set drinks before the friend and her. Vodka tonic, bottle of Amstel Light. He was tall and thin, not young, not old. He hadn't brought her a glass but asked if she needed one. She didn't.
 She liked to swig straight from the bottle. Liked the way it burned down her throat with the burning settling deep into her neck glands. "That gills feeling," she called it. She sat on a high stool along the short arm of the long, long wooden L bar, next to the friend who sucked on a skinny blue straw while she checked out a surfer dude wearing a Chlorox-white T-shirt.
 It was Sunday night. And it felt good to be out on a Sunday night. She studied the bartender. He was alone behind the bar, busy whipping up every sort of drink without any too-quick, jerky movements. His oatmeal flannel shirt glided up and down the inside bar like a dust rag. Despite his height and boniness, his coloring was as worn and soft as the flannel. Work-shirt blue eyes. Cautious eyes that had seen a lot. Remembered, too. Eyes she kept catching on her.
 On the big screen TV in back near the pool room, *Lady Sings the Blues* was starting, and Diana Ross, as Billie, was a plain, awkward girl.
 Surf boy was ignoring the friend, and her entire face, with its strong bones and almond-shaped eyes, conveyed her displeasure. She glared at him over her shoulder, patted her closely-cropped hair, and pronounced, "Guys who look like him are always pond scum."
 "Just the type you go for."
 "Exactly," the friend confirmed.
 The pond scum in question was edging toward a girl standing at the bar cornerpoint. She had a heart-shaped face and small, heart-

shaped, red lips to match. She sipped at a pale green liquid from a dainty cocktail glass. She was very young and had the delicate features of a painted doll — the kind you collect on a shelf because their arms and legs don't move. Men moved around her like sharks, pretending to veer this way and that, but never really digressing from the imaginary ring of which she was the center. The girl acted oblivious to their fins. That's what girls like that do — remain serene and cool and never guzzle beer out of the bottle.

While she studied the girl, a fresh Amstel appeared. She mouthed "thanks" to the bartender as people behind her yelled drink orders into her hair.

He was at the bar midpoint washing glasses and watching her with sidelong glances. He washed two glasses at a time, dunking each in two soap-filled mini sinks, then in a third clear one for rinsing.

She'd smile when she caught him looking, and he'd smile too. He looked younger, even gentler, when he smiled. Softened, like the sandy-gray hair that sat atop his head as curly and temporary as sea foam. She wondered why he wasn't ogling the heart-faced girl.

She had never looked like Heartface, not in her twenties, not now, not ever. But that was OK; her arms and legs did move. And she'd already spent some time on a shelf of her own.

She sighed. More like a cliff ledge. A place you end up when you climb and you try and you climb and you never make everyone happy and there's nowhere left to go. So she'd leapt onto a San Fran-bound plane, run away. For five days, anyway.

She wouldn't think now; she'd let her eyes scan for distractions. There were lots. Surf boy gave up on Heartface and joined a mutually blond, tan, neon-clad group at a large table along the wall. The twenty-something crowd seemed to be split amongst beach, grunge or flower children.

Several thirty-to-fortyish yuppies sporting Ralph Lauren polos and madras bermudas passed through en route to the jazz band upstairs. They never stayed. Others, older but not yuppie, donned biker leather, colorful ethnic gauze or retro bell-bottoms grounded by chunky-heeled boots.

She happily clicked together the thick heels of her own freshly-purchased boots on the rung of her stool. She wondered how people were classifying her, how she would label herself.

The friend had laughed all day about the boots.

"You're actually going to wear those in Springfield?"

"You bet."

"Take pictures. I want to see the looks you get."

"How about a picture of that?" she asked, pointing with her chin to a trio of Hispanic men just inside the door. Their hair was as black and shiny as their leather jackets. Though they talked and moved as friends, two of them were merely entourage to the one. He stood between them, casually netting the scene with huge, round eyes the color of the dark beer in his hand. He wore silver earrings and rings like gypsy royalty. The silver absorbed what little light there was; earrings and rings played catch with it each time he took a drink.

This light interplay made it even harder to quit staring. She had to laugh when she finally looked away and saw gaping eyes and mouths everywhere, like dead fish.

The bartender watched her laugh as he shook a plasma-red mixture. Poured it, served it, rang it and returned to his post opposite her.

"Diana Ross doesn't look anything like Billie Holiday," he announced.

"Doesn't sing like her either, but I still like this movie."

He peeked over his shoulder at the screen without really looking, then down at the bar between them.

"You really live in Illinois?"

"I really do. Springfield," she confirmed.

"You don't look like you do."

"And how does someone from Illinois look?"

"Beats me. I'm from Madison, Wisconsin."

"She should be here." The friend interrupted their laughing. "Shouldn't she?"

"Maybe." He paused. "Everybody here tries too hard to be cool, to be different." He paused again. "You seem different without trying. I don't know." He shrugged and laughed.

She slumped slightly on her stool, hiding her eyes behind her Amstel bottle.

"You should move here," the friend reiterated. "Pack up your kids, your stuff, and throw away any map with Springfield on it — that's what I did."

"Where are the restrooms?" she asked, already standing and edging away.

She made her way toward the back, walking the length of the bar, almost never looking across it. Even so, she glimpsed her reflection amidst all the nameless faces in the long bar mirror. She didn't look the way she'd envisioned herself. She never did.

"Oh who cares!" she said out loud to Billie Holiday, who smiled back as she happily sang in a Harlem night club.

Some guys in the pool room heard her and snickered as she headed into the little bathroom. It had only two stalls, and one of them was out of commission. She stepped into line with trepidation, aware of her new boots absorbing murky water.

"Why don't the guys' toilets ever overflow?" someone asked.

"They'd just piss in the sink," a voice answered from the one working stall.

Giggles echoed throughout the marshy room. Even the heart-faced girl's pouty mouth turned up a little before she checked herself in the mirror and fluffed her long, blond, curly hair. The girl didn't even need to do that.

When the line moved her face to face with the mirror, she scowled and thought, "You look as old as you are." Bathroom flourescents could be so cruel. She considered reapplying lipstick, but it would only come off on her beer bottle.

Flushing after her turn, she watched the bowl water threaten, touching the rim before slowly diminishing.

Back out in the middle of things, she weaved through the crowd. Watching Billie H. flirt with Billy Dee Williams made her run into the doorman. The two towers of glass in his hands didn't even tremble.

"Here," he said to the bartender. "You guys seem short-handed."

"Thanks," the bartender replied, grabbing the empties, then going into his three-sink dunking routine once more. "We forgot about the holiday tomorrow."

The doorman wasn't nearly as big or burly as bouncers usually were. Not at all. He had just enough American Indian in him to yield bone-straight hair the color of tar and a nose shaped like an arrowhead. She could easily imagine his profile minted into a silver dollar, looking a hell of a lot better than Ike. He padded about unassumingly. Unlike the gypsy prince, he seemed to have no idea how beautiful he was. Even Heartface cast a cool, long-lashed gaze in his direction.

Back at their bar niche, the friend examined the first set of photos they had taken in the old black-and-white photo booth nestled in an alcove kitty-corner to their seats.

The friend pointed to a shot on the strip. "I like this one of me."

"I look like a ghost!" she whined.

"You do! Look, you don't even have a nose in this one. Let's have another drink, then take some more."

"OK, but let's pull the background curtain this time. I'd like to show up as more than an apparition."

"Deal. Hail the bartender, why don't you; he's looking for excuses to talk to you."

"He's just friendly."

"Right. That's why we haven't paid for a single drink."

She raised a finger at the bartender, and he came over with reinforcements. "We need more drinks to help us bulk up for another photo session."

"I've found there to be a correlation between drinking and creative posing. Show me all of your pictures at the end of the night, so I can study the progression."

"Purely for scientific research, right?"

"Well, of course," he said, smiling.

The friend stood abruptly. "I want to buy her a shot — preferably something that'll make her produce melanin. Quickly." She snickered and added, "Now I must pee and practice some new faces."

"Good! Get outta here!"

"She's a lot of fun — says you've known each other since college."

"Yep. She's from Springfield too, though she rarely admits it."

"That's nice, you know, when a friendship grows, along with the people. She comes in here when she's alone — we hang out — kind of be alone together."

"She says you're a painter."

"Painter-slash-bartender — like everyone else in San Francisco. You an artist, too?"

"No, I write some."

"I knew, something — you watch people like you drink — slow sips."

"I'm just nosy."

"Me too. Then I spit out what I absorbed into a big, weird painting — even too weird for here. That's why I want to move to Hawaii. Maui. Just live in a hut near the beach and paint."

"Hey man!" another bartender called. "We got a lot of thirsty people here!"

"Coming!" he called back. Then, "Do you like melon balls?"

"Yes I do."

"Coming right up. Can't guarantee it will give you color, though," he teased.

She stared him down a minute, then warned, "Don't make me come back there."

"Go ahead." He called her bluff. "I could use the help." He extended his fingers at her in sort of a wave, and he was off.

"Did you get a load of that doorman!" The friend was back, wide-eyed with an erect straw between her perfect white teeth.

"Gorgeous."

"And really nice, too. He helped me make my juke box selections, and I could barely maintain enough composure to press the right buttons." She inhaled deeply and fanned herself with her hand. "I played 'Chloe Dancer' for you."

"I love that song, but it's a when-you're-feelin'-low kind of tune."

"How festive . . . let's take more pictures, then."

Inside the teeny old booth, sharing the single stool, they made laughing, contorted faces in the medicine-cabinet-sized mirror. They had drawn the background curtain, but cheek-to-her-friend's-dark-skinned-cheek, she looked paler than ever.

"Creatures of the night!" she called out as they formed their best vampire faces for the last shot. "That bartender's pretty nice."

"He likes you."

"He's probably nice to everyone."

"He is. But I could tell by what he asked about you that he likes you."

"What'd you tell him?"

"Stuff."

"Like what?"

"Like what?! Don't be coy with me, girlfriend! And he's very intuitive, so don't try to fool him either."

"I'm not trying to fool anybody."

"Right." The friend rolled her eyes at their reflections.

"I'm not!"

"Why'd you come out here?"

"To visit you!"

The friend turned to her, looking her right in the eye. "Look, you live a script somebody else wrote. Why — I don't know. And every so often, you go off to dabble — to live a little — in the margins. Well honey, welcome to the margins."

She looked down at the grimy, wood floor. Their photo strip had shot out of the slot onto it. "I still look like a ghost."

When they returned to the bar, Heartface was gone. So was the gypsy prince. Maybe they'd found each other. Or maybe they needed to be home by midnight before their glamour evaporated.

Billie Holiday lay crumpled next to a toilet, shooting up morphine.

"Chloe Dancer" played and that sad feeling coiled around her.

At the cornerpoint of the bar where Heartface had been, the friend talked to a girl she knew. Actually, she was yelling at the girl for not using condoms with her boyfriend.

The girl was young and wild-eyed. She had long, brown hair that seemed thick and dry. She nervously brushed it from her eyes as she made excuses. When she smiled, the girl looked almost happy in a frantic way.

"Has he been tested?" she asked, leaning toward their conversation.

"Who cares!" The friend turned on her. "Around here, it's a strict 'no glove, no love' policy."

"I just thought — "

"Well don't! You're married and have no idea what it's like out here in the trenches!"

"Sorry!" she yelled, settling back in her seat.

The young girl had scurried away as soon as the focus was diverted from her. Now she sat at the other end of the bar, holding a mug of beer with both hands; her feverish eyes darted around the room in between chugs — scanning for the condomless boyfriend no doubt.

The friend continued to stand. Her face smoldered with that ferocity it exuded when she was deadly serious or had had a lot to drink.

"We missed last call, didn't we?" she said more to herself than to the friend.

"Want another?" the bartender asked, seeming to appear from nowhere.

"Can I?"

He slipped her last Amstel Light before her and stayed and talked as everyone else was being herded out the door.

When he moved away for a moment to collect some empties, the friend whispered, "Cool! We get to stay! Keep talking; I'm going to see if the doorman needs any help tidying up." She followed the last line with some wicked tittering as she stood and smoothed her clothes and hair.

The bartender motioned to her from the center of the long part. He was on the outside of the bar, now.

They sat on side-by-side stools, and it was a bit startling to look into the long bar mirror that held only them. Not even the friend, trying to sweep the doorman with a huge push broom, was visible in it. Even more surprising was how their conversation didn't ebb. They flipped through each other's lives, pausing only at the underlined good parts and to share her last cigarette.

He really did want out of San Francisco. He was weary of the constant migration, the disappointed, the homeless. Even the energy. He felt for San Francisco what she felt for Springfield, and discontentment lapped between them until she didn't know where his ended and hers began.

"Maui will be different. So much better. Simpler. I've just got to get there."

She started to lodge one of her standard complaints, and she saw her mouth open in the mirror. But instead of forming words, it remained agog as her collage life flashed in one panoramic moment. And it wasn't a bad one or even in a bad place. No . . . it was a ghost town marriage that'd let her down.

"Springfield's not that bad, I guess, if you're happy . . . "

He didn't reply. He knew too.

She turned toward the big, blank screen in back, knowing the movie was over. "Hell, Billie Holiday just wanted to get to a club downtown."

"Our cab's here." The friend called from the door.

She stood to leave. "It's been really nice talking to you." She bent to hug him goodbye.

He kissed her lightly. Then hugged her. And hugged her.

She walked out the door, into the waiting taxi without looking back or even thinking until her head rested against the worn vinyl seat. The cab sped off into the opaque night. Headlights cut through the darkness as if it were still, with nothing beneath the surface. The friend stared out into the blackness. She just closed her eyes, trying to imagine what it was like in Maui.

Bonnie Madison

◆

Poems

Big

When you're big
For your age,
You avoid bumping
Into people.

You open doors,
You take no credit
For being twelve
In the ninth grade.

All the other girls
Have a smug secret
In the bathroom,
And on shower day,
You blush in your
White cotton undershirt.

You dream of
Orphanages you might run,
Or people saved
By your strength,
You walk your friends
Home on dark streets
And return alone,
Smiling.

Bypassing Toronto

In the center lane
Semis suck my marrow.
In the left
The road leads
Into a wall where
Another driver
Releases me.
On the cassette
Horowitz reminds me
That he was afraid, too.

Cities are wasteful,
Unfit for the honor
Of my spending,
The countryside,
Conservative.
It does not want me.

Too well packed for an
Unplanned trip, I wait
To be guided,
To surround some
Sensibility,
Which I know
Must be my own.

Visit to a Country Home

He leaves it often, he
tells me, to walk the
shopping mall — its fluor-
escent lights and cobble
stones break the
monotony of his life.

I visit his home place,
once rich with dark woods,
faded linoleum, a legged
and skirted sink under
open windows, re-

placed by new blond edges on
sofas, windows, walls. Nothing
old bleeds through the thick
sculptured carpets of its floors.
It is sealed shut, air con-
ditioned, the cellar stairs
covered by a carpeted
trap door: I see its ring.

Outdoors, tall oaks
condescend the tree-
lined road rolling through
Illinois hills of corn and
beans, mown fields.
Cicadas strum their
ancient tune.

Gladys

Gladys sold underwear
for Monkey-Wards, kept the
order books at night,
moved the stock from shelves to
bins 'til her back gave out.
I saw her different under the
high tin ceilings, her hustle
prouder than at home.

Exclusive dealer to the deaf, she
spoke their way on fingers that later
spelled "enough," her name in Wards was
Madison — Dad's name, her respect.

She introduced me to her gang,
I tall and loose beside her
starched pride. Suppers
she served us cake from
B. & Z., and talked like only
Dad had talked before.

Amputee

This morning he
Called me
Up from that place
Which shunned him,
His voice as real
In my mind's ear
As the rings gone,
Pulled from the finger
Where no air touches —
A severed limb's pain
Buried in the vault.

Knitting

The wine wool
spills at my side.
Taking the stitches
out by dim light I
hope to put them
right again not
start over. Casting
on is hard — to get
the right tension.

It is just a matter of
pulling one loop
through another, one
at a time. He
will never stay.

Memorial Garden 6/87
For Brother

Beyond a wreath of
worn stones, broken
near a fountain and
facing a small water,
its horizon spiked with
masts, their sails furled,
there is a workman's bucket
overturned.

Here also is a grove of
oaks, their sighs like
that of water
washing.

Bonnie Madison

◆

The Party (A Play in One Act)

CAST: ROSIE
HAYZOOS
AT LEAST A DOZEN PEOPLE OF VARIOUS AGES,
COLORS AND BODY TYPES.

SCENE ONE

There is an old wooden table (no tablecloth) center stage. A small apartment stove and oven, old sink with curtain below, dishes drying in a wooden rack, wicker couch filled with pillows and lace curtains are around the periphery of the stage. At least one curtain is blowing toward the room. There are a bowl of chips and a container of dip at the corner of the table. Two people, a man and a woman, sit at the table across from each other and perpendicular to the audience (they are seen in profile). There are poker cards and chips on the table. The man is thin but muscular, dark complected, a little unkempt, beard (optional), long hair in ponytail. The woman has on long, artsy earrings, a silk jacketed suit. She is well-rounded, average height.

ROSIE: Hit me. I need one, just one.

Hayzoos gives her a card without comment.

ROSIE: *(Mumbling.)* Oh, yes! *(Louder.)* Have some chips and dip, Hayzoos. The turkey's almost ready. Doesn't it smell good? *(She looks toward the oven.)* I'll cook the potatoes as soon as this hand is over.

Hayzoos grunts assent.

ROSIE: I bet two. *(Throws chips in center.)* Are you gonna call?

HAYZOOS: I'll raise you one and call.

ROSIE: *(Lays down her cards.)* Two pair — jacks and nines.

HAYZOOS: Full house.

ROSIE: Oh, you won again. How do you do it? You have such a poker face. *(Reaches across the table and takes his hands in hers.)* I love your hands so strong and your arms. Where'd you get this scar?

HAYZOOS: I've forgotten. It's been there a long time.

ROSIE: Well, I'm going to peel the potatoes and get them boiling. Is anyone else coming? I love parties, always have. I'll read you the story about my first party sometime. My sister gave it for my tenth birthday. She was late because she saw a dead man by the tracks and the party was really different, but it was a hoot.

HAYZOOS: I'd like to hear it. I expect Tom and Bill and maybe Mary and Sarah. I'm sure there will be more. Don't worry about food. Everyone brings some.

ROSIE: *(Moves to the oven and opens it and begins basting the turkey.)* Look how brown it is. Oh, smell that! I used a new recipe for the stuffing — sage and bread and apples, prunes, celery, a little onion. Sound good?

HAYZOOS: I'm sure it'll be great. You're a good cook, Rosie.

ROSIE: *(Brings a newspaper, bag of potatoes, pan and peeler to the table and begins to peel.)* I've been writing, especially in the morning.

HAYZOOS: I know everyone will want to hear you read tonight.

ROSIE: I'd be glad to, honey. You always make me feel so good. How long have we known each other?

HAYZOOS: A long time, Rosie.

ROSIE: How come Bill and Tom are coming? Have I ever met them?

HAYZOOS: Yeah, you entered a dance contest with Bill. Think you did the rumba.

ROSIE: Oh, yeah. I wore my green print gathered skirt and that peasant blouse that I gave to Rita when I outgrew it. But I wasn't any good. Poor Bill, he would have won with a better partner. But you didn't say why they're coming.

HAYZOOS: The plague.

ROSIE: Oh, poor Bill. That fucking plague. But all's well . . . I don't know how many potatoes to peel. I guess the whole bag. Then if they aren't all eaten, I'll make potato pancakes later. Will you be here for breakfast? They're good with huevos. *(She continues peeling, placing peeled potatoes in the pan, then goes to the sink to fill the pan with water. She sets the pan on the stove to cook.)*

HAYZOOS: Probably. Don't worry, there'll be plenty for everyone.

SCENE TWO

The table is set with a turkey and bowls of food. Leaves have been added. Guests begin arriving in various forms of dress: Dahktis, love beads, suits, evening gowns, jeans and sweatshirts, military uniforms, corduroys and penny loafers. There are conventional types, professorial types, housewives, telephone linemen. Rosie stands at a framed doorway (no door) near the blowing curtain, greeting each person with a hug and a comment.

ROSIE: Sweetheart! I'm so glad you came! *(Moves around the room between greeting guests to see that party foods are put in bowls and set on small tables.)*

Guests begin helping themselves, rearranging the furniture, getting bowls from cupboards, beers out of the refrigerator, talking loudly about all manner of subjects: esoteric, practical, intellectual, banal. There are a lot of hugs exchanged. Conversations are extemporaneous for each performance of the play. There are also a few who retreat to corners or to chairs or the couch and watch the others. Hayzoos walks around the room, his arm on shoulders, looking into eyes, relatively quiet himself. In between, he pours wine and passes it around. Rosie continues greeting new arrivals with hugs and comments.

ROSIE: Honey, you look great!

GUEST: I feel great, too!

ROSIE: Angel, didn't you bring the baby?

GUEST: Not tonight. Next time, Rosie.

ROSIE: Bob! It wouldn't be a party without you!

GUEST: Rosie, I might have known you'd still be having parties. I wouldn't miss one of your parties.

She begins enjoying the party more like a guest herself, moving from group to group, eating snacks and drinking wine. Guests begin greeting people at the door with hugs and comments.

GUEST: Dick, you made it. Have you read Sartre's latest?

GUEST: Betty, saw you at the concert last week. Guess you didn't see me. Wasn't Mahler great?

GUEST: Carl, love you, man. What do you think of our Cosmos, now? *(Slaps him on the back affectionately.)*

GUEST: Anne, still writing? Read us something later? Can't wait.

GUEST: Buddy, I can't tell you how sorry I am. I wasn't there for you. Please forgive me. *(Long hug.)*

Greeters' comments shouldn't stand out much more than the conversations at the party. Conversations should overlay so the audience may not be able to comprehend all that's being said. All conversation must be positive, and joking tempered with expressions of love such as that to Carl. It should be noisy for about five minutes.

GUEST: She's the best baby. Sleeps all night.

GUEST: We got that vote through the house. It was close, but the shelters are open twenty-four hours, fully staffed, now.

After about five minutes of conversation, all begin to pull chairs out from the table. All guests must fit at the table or at TV trays or card tables added to the end of the table. No one sits apart. All begin eating and it is quiet for at least one minute. Conversation begins slowly again, but much more quietly, with only one person talking at a time.

GUEST: This is wonderful, Rosie.

ROSIE: Thank you, honey. It's a new recipe.

GUEST: This is the best wine!

Hayzoos lifts a wine bottle and motions for the guest to pass a goblet. The goblet is passed and refilled and sent back down the table.

GUEST: Ella, you gonna sing for us later?

GUEST: Love to, baby.

After more impromptu conversation, chairs are pushed back, guests carry their own plates to stack at the sink, leaves are taken out of the table as conversations continue simultaneously. Rosie and others begin setting out desserts and coffee cups. Members of the cast go into the audience with exclamations similar to those at the beginning of the party. The house lights are turned on. The party gradually grows from the stage into the audience. Desserts and coffee and tea, sugar and cream are carried out to the audience. Audience members are involved in helping to carry out card tables and food. If possible, audience chairs are put aside. Stage crew and make up artists are involved now also.

CAST MEMBER: I love your dress! Come join us!

CAST MEMBER: You have a beautiful smile. Please come and have dessert.

CAST MEMBER: Are you enjoying the evening? Thanks so much for coming. Please come join the party.

Cast members practice compliments during rehearsals and ask audience members to join the party. All members of the audience who are amenable are included. Goodbyes begin with hugs and pats on the back. Audience members are guided toward the exits or toward the coat racks with comments.

CAST MEMBER: We're so glad you came. Come back soon.

CAST MEMBER: Be happy.

CAST MEMBER: Love ya!

CAST MEMBER: You're always welcome! Come anytime!

The play is over when all audience members have exited the building.

Debra Nickelson Smith

◆

The Deal (From *The Long Sneak*)

"Hey, Charcie, wait up!" I heard Trace shout over the students in the corridor. It was Monday morning, not even nine o'clock, and I had three minutes to make it from my eight o'clock composition class to the *emergency* faculty meeting.

"Hi, Trace. I don't have my checkbook."

"Charcie." Trace grinned. "Got time for coffee?"

"Not today, Trace. Emergency faculty meeting in two minutes."

"Emergency? What do you figure, Charcie? Sex, drugs, loan-sharking?"

"Maybe," I said. "One can only hope."

"I've got a splitting headache."

"So you had fun at the Ritz-Carlton?" I asked.

"An absolute blast. Got any aspirin?"

"Here," I said, fishing my keys out of my jacket pocket. "The top drawer of the tan file cabinet, and stay out of the prescription stuff, okay?"

"Me, unlawful? Never," Trace said with angelic inflection.

"Right."

"I really don't need to borrow any money. It's just that I'm temporarily out of cash, and they won't give me a cup of coffee unless I give them — hey, why don't you propose the cafeteria start taking credit cards?"

"What?" Why fight it, I thought. I rummaged through my purse, found my billfold and three five dollar bills. I handed Trace one of them. "Wait for me in my office, bring me my change, and remember Stafford College is a smoke-free environment."

"Hey, you oughtta have a meeting about that."

"Trace, what are you doing here so damned early?"

"Gotta talk to you — kind of urgent — it'll take five minutes tops."

"You've got two ex-husbands, both of them doctors. Why are you always borrowing money from me?"

"I didn't come here to borrow money, except for the one dollar because your cafeteria doesn't take plastic. I'm desperately in need of caffeine. Shit. I don't know. Maybe if I had a better lawyer. It all just slips through my fingers. And being a P.I. doesn't pay all that great. The pay is fine if everybody paid, but only about half of them do, and collecting from the other half ain't exactly inexpensive."

"Here comes the head cheese," I whispered as we reached the auditorium door. "Better get my butt in there."

"Does he always walk like that? You can tell a lot by a walk."

"Like what?"

"Like he's got a cob up his ass, a tick digging its head into the rectal tissues, a severe dystension of the perineal wall, acute hemorrhoids at the very least."

"Not so loud, Trace. I *work* here. Wait for me in my office, okay?"

"Deal."

As I sat down in the damp chill of the auditorium, I felt the pit of my stomach sink.

Something was bothering Trace, something more than just money. And she was right about the chief administrator. He was a first class asshole. At least the "emergency" meeting was something I could sleep through: preferential parking policies and a revision of insurance benefits. I half envied Trace, the varied nature of her profession, the divorce surveillance that led her to Chicago's Ritz-Carlton for the weekend, even if she got stuck with the bill.

When I got back to my office, there was Trace in her skin-tight size-five black denims by Calvin, taupe silk Liz Claiborne jacket and blouse, and stiletto-heeled Gucci boots resting on top of my desk. In her hand she held a compact camera with a long narrow lens that was zooming rhythmically forward and back.

"How much do you think this weighs?" she asked, zoom out, zoom in.

"I don't know."

The lens erupted and recoiled three more times.

"About five pounds?" I guessed, hoping she would stop burning the zoom function batteries. "Stop doing that. It's getting to me."

"What does it remind you of?" Trace pressed again, this time running it up and down even more compulsively.

"If that camera was a dog, my leg would be wet."

Trace beamed, revealing her Hollywood smile. She leaned forward, handing me the camera. "Five pounds? You're not even close. That's what your old Pentaxes would weigh with a Vivitar telephoto. You'd need a tripod for that."

"It's so light!" I said in disbelief.

"One pound, three ounces. It'll fit in your pocket. State of the art Japanese technology."

"Are you selling them?" I asked.

"Not on your — I just thought you might want to play with it, try it out. You're the one that taught me how to use a camera," Trace said as she massaged her right temple in a circular motion.

"Hey, did you find something for your headache?" I asked as I glanced at the tan file cabinet.

"There's nothing in there — a bottle of Darvon that expired in 1988, some vintage 1993 Valium — are you saving this stuff for a special occasion?"

I opened the top drawer. "You missed a bottle of infant Tylenol."

"So?"

"It doesn't expire until 1998, cherry flavored — it's the same as the adult stuff, just not as concentrated." I handed her the bottle.

"Won't your kids need that?"

"They're too sophisticated. Have to have the chewable tablets."

"Cherry, huh?"

"Yeah."

Trace eyed it suspiciously. "Looks like Mercurochrome."

"God, are we old," I heard myself saying.

"How much should I try?"

"Oh, I don't know — half a bottle?"

Trace raised the bottle to her lips, tipped it, swallowed, and winced. "It tastes like Mercurochrome. Yuck. No wonder your kids switched to chewable."

"You tasted Mercurochrome?"

"Only once. I was three or four. Didn't you?"

"No," I said flatly.

"I did. I tried evergthing. Most *recovering* adults — even when we were kids — I was curious. I'd drain the last two drops out of my stepdad's beer cans. If anybody set down a glass I grabbed it. I tried everything in the medicine cabinet, including some of my Aunt Elsa's Elavil — I thought they were M&Ms. I slept for two days. There ought to be twelve-step programs for kids. That's where it all starts."

Trace tipped the bottle of infants' Tylenol to her lips, swallowed twice, winced and said, "I quit. My head doesn't hurt that bad."

"So how much did that camera cost? I'm curious."

"Eleven hundred used, but it's deductible."

"That's more than the book value of my car."

"But Charcie, your car's a lot more useful — and it's got *character* — I love the old ghetto cruisers — like walking backwards in time. Too bad you can't buy eight tracks anymore."

"My grandmother wore it out anyway — listening to Jerry Vale and Sinatra — *I did it my way.* "

"Speaking of *his way,* what did cob-up-the-ass have on his mind?

Will a cost of living raise be reflected in your next contract?"

"Shit, no," I said, exhausted. "We're just damned lucky to have any kind of insurance. It's insuring the seculars that's breaking the back of this institution, or so they say. It certainly isn't the contracted salaries. The nuns and priests are insured by the church. They can't accept wages."

"That's what it takes," Trace conjectured. "A bunch of you missionaries pulling together. You might save half of these kids."

"I'm *not* a missionary," I asserted.

"Yes you are, Charcie. Not one hustling the religious doctrine, but you are hustling. It's in your walk. Hell, I was one of your students. I never gave a crap about poetry or drama until you conned me. And just maybe it kept me from sliding off the edge again. You walk into a classroom like you've just won the Lottery and you're going to share it with every student. What a hustle."

"That was fifteen years ago," I said. "I was young then."

"You've still got the same walk."

"Fifteen years ago," I sighed. "You know, I've got a student that reminds me of you back then. She's missed the last four classes. I hope she's okay. I called the foundation. She's in third phase of drug rehab. They couldn't tell me anything — part of her work release agreement. I don't suppose you'd like a missing person case, if I could afford you."

"Let me tell you about missing persons," Trace said soberly, her green eyes narrowed to a Clint Eastwood set of slits. "Most of them are just people who don't want to be found. Let me tell you about dopeheads — been there, got the T-shirts. Maybe something might have happened to her, but personally, I think there's an excellent chance that she's just being a shit."

"I hope you're right."

"Tell you what — tell you what. I still know someone at the foundation, a board member, who just happens to owe me a small favor. Why don't I call him up and see if he'd like to meet me for coffee."

"I'll pay you," I volunteered enthusiastically. "I guess that's what they all say, but I really will."

"Hold it, Charcie," Trace said with a knowing smile. "Who said anything about calling in the I.R.S. on this?"

"The I.R.S.?" I asked. "I didn't know you could leave them out."

"Of course you can, Charcie. As long as no money changes hands, who cares?"

"I care. Besides, I'm not asking you to do it for free."

Trace grinned like the Cheshire cat. "And I'm not exactly offering to. Charcie, can't we just swap favors? Politicians do it all the time. If a tree falls in the forest and there is no one there to hear it, did it make a sound?"

"Don't get me started. I'll lose sleep over *that*. Okay. So, uh, you'll do something for me, and . . . I'll do something for you, and . . . neither of us will serve time?"

"Precisely. I do it all the time. Doctors do it for other doctors. They comp the fees for services as a professional courtesy."

I swallowed hard. "Okay. What do you want me to do?"

"Photography."

"Photography? I broke up my darkroom six years ago. Half of it's in boxes in my brother's basement."

Trace held up the diminuitive spy camera. "I'm not looking for Ansel Adams. And I just need *one* picture, taken between 5:30 and 6:00 on Tuesday evening — "

"That's my night class. I'll be here eating a ham sandwich and reviewing my lecture notes."

"I know you will. All you have to do is point this out your window, wait for a blonde lady in a black BMW and *click*."

"That's all?" I asked.

"That's all. Are we talking a deal?"

I took a deep breath through my nose and slowly exhaled through my circularly shaped lips. I was back in Lamaze.

"It's a deal," I said hesitantly.

"Okay. Now what's the name of this lost little puppy dog?"

"Mary Therese Linden. Everyone calls her Tess."

"What's she look like?"

"About my size, five-foot-five, a hundred and fifteen pounds, auburn hair, blue-green eyes, nineteen years old. She's a beautiful young woman."

"I'll see what I can do," Trace said as her watch beeped. "Oh shit," she said, shutting it off. "Meeting a client for lunch at the country club. Gotta run. Here's two rolls of film, the instruction book. Have fun with it. Take some shots of your kids, save one frame for me."

"Are you sure I won't screw this up, Trace? Why not just do it yourself?"

"Got a hot date. Someone I haven't seen in two years is coming through town. I'm making lasagna and chocolate mousse. The Do Not Disturb sign might get hung on the door, if you get my drift. Ciao." She smiled and slipped through my door.

I had the feeling there was a lot she wasn't telling me. What she didn't know was that there was something I wasn't telling her. As I watched her red Volvo leave the visitor parking lot, I remembered my five dollars. By tomorrow I would forget it again.

Roberta DeKay

Poems

**And Another Woman Leaves Ireland
(for Anna Kelly Gill)**

The hair is pulled back,
pinned out of sight;
the skin is flawless and smooth.
The eyebrows
arch up perfectly
from the bridge of her nose
as though brushed by a skilled artist.
The eyes look
somewhere to her right
not toward the photographer.

I've searched my grandmother's face
for answers and clues
for over twenty-five years.
Some days the oval picture
seems more a hand-mirror
reflecting back my own face
and at times
it seems the face of a writer,
but one who did not leave a word.

Even the names of her parents
were not spoken or passed down
to her children —
I found them on her death certificate,
hidden as runes, but runes
that caused tears.

I wonder if this picture was taken
the week you arrived?
Did your mother, Ellen,
stand with your father, Patrick,
on the pier at Cobh to watch
the ship head off to the States?
Or like some
I've read about,
did she fall to the ground,
pulling her hair and crying?
And did you call back
with the lightness of youth,
"I'll write, I'll send a picture,
I'll be fine."
I even went there you know,
to that very pier
looking toward my homeland
while standing on yours. Maybe
I hoped for a vision, a word, a clue
toward your feelings that day,
but instead I walked
the new museum
glad your parents had not been victims
of the famine or passengers on
coffin ships.

I have scanned
your clothing for any hint:
a stylish dress with velvet trim
around the collar
and sleeves
that move out like opening wings.

At your throat, an anchor pin glitters
like a symbol of hope
in life's sea. Perhaps your parents
gave it to you as a farewell gift,
one I'd like to hold,
fasten it some morning
to a dress knowing your story

so I could begin
to protect you forever
from the innocence
of your own eyes.

Belief and the Blooming Jacaranda Trees

I can believe flowers bloomed
in the wake of the Buddha's footsteps.

I can believe Moses' desert weary feet
never walked the Promised Land,

but his dying eyes were still ablaze
from that Face to face encounter with God.

I can believe Jesus felt strength
flow from his body when the

perservering yet bleeding woman
touched the hem of his garment.

I can believe Einstein
could not believe the universe was moving
constantly outward.

I can believe he
changed the equation to hide
the unthinkable for years.

I can believe Mary Magdalene's tears
washed her master's feet completely,

and her thick black hair fell forward
in one erotic and whole moment.

I can believe Our Lady of Czestochowa
saw something so sad, yet so divine,
her heart broke in two.

I can believe all this and much more
since that early June morning

when I walked across the lawn in the shade
of the blooming Jacaranda trees. Looking back
I saw my footprints as bright green pools

on a purple cloth, and the soles of my feet
I held up to the sunlight
were abloom with purple Jacaranda flowers.

Sonya Tolstoy

There must have been fire
in her almost blind eyes
when she stood up from
her everyday solitude
by the fireplace —

stood up to give orders
to grown sons and daughters,
telling her son
to call the commissioner
and have him send troops
to defend Tolstoy's papers and estate;
orders to her old cook
who had been fat in Sonya's youth,
now thin in his new freedom.
"How to arm the peasants?" he had asked.
"With pitchforks and scythes," she replied.

Then she kept them
silent through the night,
this woman they had thought senile,
this woman who copied *War and Peace*
by hand six times over
in her candlelit room.

In the daylight, Yasna Polyanna
stood untouched along the road
where Red Flags flew from housetops
all the way to Moscow.

just how frightening
could the Bolsheviks be
for a woman
who tried to keep
Tolstoy in line
for more than fifty years!

Something Holy

On the San Tomas Expressway
where eight lanes of traffic come
to a stop
like one giant engine,
there came
into the peripheral vision of my right eye
the Indian woman
in a shimmering blue sari
which covered her black hair
like a wish.

Across those eight lanes
she moved so softly;
her whole body merely
a whisper hidden in folds of
shimmering blue. I strained to see
if she really had feet, if she did exist.

All those engines at a standstill!
To the left where
my eyes searched
I could not find her again,

but oh
how the air
filled
with possibility!

Linda McElroy

◆

Flight to Freeport

Maizie was a grown woman with two kids in college so she really should have known better. All week she had managed to hide her cough from Walter by drinking cough medicine and sucking on mentholated cough drops till her tongue was blue. But now shivering as a November wind swirled snowflakes through the door of the shelter, she felt the familiar tickle in the back of her throat.

Unable to help herself, she gave in to a bout of coughing that forced her down onto the icy bench.

"For Chrissakes, Maizie!" Walter said. "Why didn't you tell me you had a cold?"

"I'll be all right," she said, leaning her forehead on her suitcase. "I didn't want to ruin our second honeymoon too."

"You mean the morning sickness? You couldn't help that," Walter said, patting her shoulder.

"If only it had been just in the morning. All that wonderful food on the cruise and I couldn't keep anything down. Here comes the bus now. We'll soon be in the Bahamas and I'll feel better, I promise."

"Well, you should have worn a coat," Walter said, picking up their bags as the airport shuttle bus pulled up.

The flight from St. Louis to Miami was on time, and Maizie napped a little between interruptions by the flight attendants offering snacks, drinks and magazines. If she'd been a seasoned traveler, she would have taken advantage of that time to rest, but she didn't want to miss a second of her first flight.

A light drizzle was falling when they arrived in Miami. Although they had a two-hour layover until the flight to Freeport, they went immediately to check in. Finally, Maizie saw a small plane taxiing up to the loading gate. Mentally counting the windows, she gazed with alarm at the crowded waiting room.

"How are they going to fit all these people on that little plane?" she asked Walter.

"Those babies hold more than you think," he assured her.

But Walter was wrong.

"The four o'clock flight to Freeport has been overbooked," the check-in clerk announced. "Please come forward to board when I call your name. We'll get another plane ready for the rest of you. We're sorry for any inconvenience."

"Don't worry," Walter said. "We'll be on this flight; we were the first to check in."

But Walter was wrong.

When all the names had been called, Walter and Maizie shared the waiting room with six other disgruntled passengers for another ninety minutes.

"We're ready to board now," the clerk said. "Please bring your bags and follow me." She led the passengers down some steps and across the tarmac to a small plane that looked like a toy next to the jets pulled up to the boarding gates.

Watching two young men load their luggage into compartments in the nose, Maizie wished she had taken Walter's advice to pack light. It didn't seem safe to put all that weight in the front of the plane. I'm probably being foolish, she thought.

Just then, she noticed the pilot questioning passengers as they walked toward the plane.

"How much do you weigh?" the pilot asked each one.

"One-thirty-five," Walter said without hesitation, proud of the fact that he hadn't gained an ounce since high school.

Maizie cursed herself for signing up for this trip. She never told anyone her weight; she even shaved off a few pounds on her driver's license. But she considered the size of the plane and was afraid to lie.

"One-fifty," she mumbled, hoping Walter wouldn't hear.

"I'm sorry, ma'am. I didn't hear you," the pilot said.

"I said one-fifty," Maizie repeated, glancing at Walter, who grinned and winked at her.

The pilot began assigning seats to balance the plane. Walter sat in the back between two slim, blonde coeds. Maizie was in front of him with a chunky middle-aged lady whose husband had been seated next to the pilot. The other couple, whose weights matched, were in the two seats behind the pilot.

Since Maizie's seat was next to the door, the pilot showed her how to open it in case of an emergency and explained how to inflate the raft located under her seat.

Turning around to look at Walter, Maizie said, "This is pretty good. Only my second flight and already I'm part of the crew."

The pilot said they would be taking off as soon as he got clearance from the tower. With the propeller spinning, he taxied the plane a few yards and stopped.

Following the afternoon rain, heat and humidity began to build up inside the plane. The pilot slid open his window, but little air made its way beyond the front of the cabin. Sweat trickled down Maizie's back and sides. Wearing a sweatshirt and sweatpants had seemed like a good idea in St. Louis, but now she was uncomfortably hot. She shoved a cough drop in her mouth to try to stave off a cough, but it didn't help, and there was only one more in the package. Her cough syrup was in her suitcase, and she had to go to the bathroom. It can't be much longer, she told herself, as her seatmate pulled out a wallet fat with pictures of her grandchildren.

Jet after jet took off and landed on the runways in front of them. All the big names were there — United, American, British Airways, Quantas. It should have been fascinating to have a front-row seat for all that activity, but Maizie's head ached and she feared that another bout of coughing would make her wet herself.

The sun was turning the sky pink and violet when the pilot received clearance. The prop spun faster and faster as he revved the engine and started down the runway. Slowly the plane began to rise, and Maizie breathed a sigh of relief.

Her relief was short-lived. As the plane rose higher, her ears began to plug up. She swallowed hard trying to relieve the pressure, but the pain was almost unbearable. She opened her mouth and yawned, but that didn't help. If she hadn't started coughing, she would have whimpered in agony. Paroxysms of coughing shook her body, as Walter reached from behind her to pat her head.

"Are you all right, sweetheart?" he asked.

But Maizie was too busy coughing and trying to control her bladder to answer. She put her last cough drop in her mouth and mercifully the coughing stopped.

As twilight deepened, the engine's whir lulled the exhausted passengers to sleep. Maizie prayed that the pilot would stay awake. She wasn't sure she remembered all his instructions for dealing with an emergency.

The popping in Maizie's ears wakened her. Surprised to have drifted off, she looked out the window. The lights of Freeport glittered like loose diamonds in a black velvet case. Slowly the plane began to descend.

Gael Carnes

◆

Novel Excerpt

In the following excerpts, a sampler from a work in progress, Mary Alice must face her mother's mortality and the conflict that comes with caring for an aging parent. When her mother is found dead one morning, Mary Alice's life takes a bizarre turn. These excerpts take place before her mother's death.

Mary Alice sits at her breakfast table reading the funnies. Grey light seeps in from the window over the sink. It is raining, soft and quiet. *The Far Side* is "Graffiti in Hell." She smiles and turns the page. Travel is the next section. She has read all the rest, saving her favorite for last. This week's topic is Florida, from Tampa to Miami. Reaching for the atlas she keeps by her toaster, Mary Alice flips through the alphabet until she comes to Florida. Taking the blue highlighter clipped to the outside cover, she reads and maps a route, circling the places she would like to see — Busch Gardens, Disney World and the movie studios, St. Petersburg all the way down the gulf until she reaches Miami and the Keys.

She sips her coffee and leans back. She can almost see the palm trees and the banyans. Her family went down there together one summer and she remembers playing in the banyans, amazed by the tangled mass of shoots all anchored in the ground, a hundred trunks.

The radio announces the psychic will be on at 9:00, have your questions ready. She promised her mom that she would be there in time to listen to *Betty at Breakfast*. She takes another sip and looks out into the grey morning. She can see the top of her mother's roof, dark and wet in the rain, and the shadowed windows at the front of the house, the part for entertaining, the part they never use anymore. A James Taylor song plays; his voice is hypnotic. Mary Alice relaxes and lets it run through her. She sips the rest of the coffee, then gathers her atlas and stands. Another Saturday of laundry and cleaning and grocery shopping for her mother. Shutting off the coffeemaker, she puts on her clear plastic bonnet and a coat. When she opens her back door, the smell of heavy water and earth surround her. It is cool and the rain sounds like faded applause in the background. She locks her door and turns to the large brick house. Wiping the water from her face as she walks, she hurries across the soggy lawn to her mother's.

A house of shades. It is quiet, except for the sound of a dripping tap. She goes to the sink and twists the knobs until it stops. She walks softly in to check on her mother, to see if she is awake. She is. She lies there, eyes open in the dark room staring at the tarnished light from her window. The glass is covered with drops that gather weight and then zigzag to the sill.

"Mom, you okay?"

"Mouse. I'm fine. Just waiting for you to get here."

"How long you been up?"

"Not too long, since 7:30, I guess."

She turns her head and smiles at Mary Alice. She is never complaining. Always glad for the help. It is worse that way. When her mother never gripes or has a bad spell, it makes her feel bad because she is so weary of being there, of scheduling her life around her. Mary Alice checks her watch and goes to the radio and turns it on. She adjusts the sound so that it is loud enough to hear.

"You want some breakfast?"

"Just a few pieces of toast. First, I'd like to go to the bathroom and then sit up in the chair. I'd like to eat in the chair and look out the window."

"Sure, Mom. I should have thought of that. I'm sorry."

Her mother's body is light, full of air. It takes little strength to lift her, but Mary Alice goes slowly, taking her cues from the expressions on her mother's face. Her mom says nothing as her feet hit the floor. She grits her teeth. Her mother is proud of those teeth. They are all her own and mostly there. Every morning after breakfast and every evening before bed, Mary Alice helps her mother brush. They pause for a moment so that Mom can get a rest. Mary Alice feels her breath, the touch insubstantial, like a ghost caressing her face. A nod from her mother and they are moving, one foot pointed like a dancer's and dropped, the other pointed and dropped. Across the carpet to the open cavity of the bathroom, her mother moves, graceful in pain, determined to perform the steps. They stop while Mary Alice flips the light switch. Her mother's breath is fast and shallow. The lace at her neck swells and falls, swells and falls. There is a rail that runs along one wall of the room over the stool. Mary Alice guides her mother, waits as she claws for the metal and desperately grasps it.

"It's all right, Mouse. I can manage now. I'll call you when I'm finished."

"Sure, Mom. I'll be just outside here. I'll wait till you're set up in the chair before I get breakfast."

Her mother nods and Mary Alice shuts the door. She walks to the window. The rain is still falling. "Psychic Betty" will be on after the next news break on the radio. Another fight to ban weapons in Congress. NRA against, everyone else for. New talk of military reductions. Mary Alice breathes on the glass to steam it and draws her name in the fog. She stares at it. Somehow it is not enough. Her mother calls and she turns. She opens the door. Her mother stands holding the rail. Small tremors shake her thin body. Mary Alice wants to cry. This is not the woman she remembers, the woman who wiped the blood from scraped knees, who tucked her in at night and sang songs, who kept away the world when she didn't have sense enough to be afraid. This is not the woman. This is someone else. Someone weak and old, holding onto her mother's spirit until she is able to die. Mary Alice takes her mother's arm and guides her over to the chair by the window. Her name is fading on the glass. The psychic is coming on the radio. Her mother rests her head back and closes her eyes; she motions Mary Alice to sit.

Sitting on the bed, Mary Alice waits. The psychic is introduced. She comes on the radio twice a month on Saturdays and takes calls. One day, Betty was hit by lightning in her front yard. Since then she has had visions that have helped people find lost items, including dead bodies for the police, predict love lives, and solve job problems. All for the price of a phone call. Mary Alice listens and watches the shadows the rain makes on the carpet.

"Next caller."

"Hi, Betty."

"Hi. What can I do for you today?"

"We listen every Saturday you're on and we just love you. What I need is help finding my ring. I lost it several months ago and I can't seem to remember what I did with it."

"First of all, what's your name and your date of birth?"

"Dorothy, but my friends call me Dodo. I was born on leap year, February 29."

"Uh-huh, well, Dodo. I see the ring in a tin box or a box of some sort. Do you have anything like that?"

"No. No, I don't."

Mary Alice looks at her mom. Her face is still; her whole body leaning forward to listen. The rain falls harder outside and the sound of it hitting the roof fills the room. Mary Alice scoots back on the bed and leans against the wall. Her shoes hang over the edge. Before her mother got sick, she would never let anyone sit on the beds in street clothes.

"How about a wood-lined closet?"

"Yes, yes. I have one in the laundry room."

"Do you have a lot of laundry stored in there that you may have handled in the last few months, maybe changing seasons?"

"No, wait, yes, yes I do."

"Well, I'm getting a very strong picture of a ring nestled in soft fabric, silk or something. I think if you look there, you probably will find what you're looking for."

"Thanks, Betty. I'll do that. Right now. Thanks again."

The announcer breaks in with talk about Betty's appearances in the coming weeks. Mary Alice shifts positions. She talks to her mother while the show goes to a commercial. Her mother sits back in her chair. Her fingers are wrapped together. They are bent and crooked across her stomach.

"Sounds like intelligent guesswork to me. I could find things too if I asked enough questions."

Her mother shakes her head.

"She finds bodies for the police, Mouse. She has found people no one else could find. Can't ask the dead questions."

"I bet what she said was so general that they couldn't help but find similarities."

"Shhh-h!"

Her mother leans forward again and the psychic takes another call. Mary Alice thinks of all the things she could be doing to clean the house. The daylight shows more cobwebs across the walls and ceilings. Dust lies on the bedstand and the dresser. Mary Alice rises, the energy building inside her. She wonders what her mother does when she is like that. How does she cope? Betty has just predicted the future success of an aspiring romance writer if she sticks with it. Mary Alice walks over to her mom and rubs one bony shoulder.

"Mom, why do you listen to this stuff?"

Her mother shrugs.

"Thought I might call."

Mary Alice lets go of the shoulder and kneels down next to her mother. She takes hold of the hand and strokes it.

"What would you ask?"

"If she can see an end to this for me."

"Mom!"

"I'm serious. Don't tell me you aren't as tired of this as I am, Mouse."

Placing the hand back into her mom's lap, Mary Alice stands and kisses her on the cheek. The skin is dry, but soft.

"I love you. You know that. I want to take care of you."

Her mother sighs and waves her hand as if to shoo her away.

"I know you do; I know."

"How 'bout the toast?"

Her mother nods and leans forward in her chair. Betty is telling about a career choice for the caller's young college student. Mary Alice walks through the dark room and stops at the door. Her mother is etched against the grey light, avidly listening to the spirit of the radio. Mary Alice watches and wishes she could help her mother. It is all she can do to make tea and toast. Maybe a little laundry. She turns and goes into the kitchen.

It is a crisp morning. The rain is gone. Mary Alice squints, letting the deep green of the grass fill her vision. Her mother is saying her name; she can hear her but cannot make her neck turn or her eyes move. She is stigmatized by the fresh sunlight.

"I don't think I'll order the breakfast bar. I never eat enough to make it worth my while."

Across the way, a car turns into the parking lot. A woman gets out. She pulls a child from the backseat and hurries into the tire store. The child loses his balance as she walks, but she pulls him along anyway, yanking his arm and lifting him up off the ground. Mary Alice turns from the window.

"What did you say, Mom? I wasn't listening. I'm sorry."

Her mother sits slumped in her wheelchair, forearms on the table edge, menu in front of her. There are brown spots on the once white skin of her hands and arms. It makes Mary Alice sad. Another visible reminder that her mother is changing. Her mother sighs.

"I said I don't eat enough to make the breakfast bar worth it, so you don't have to worry about fixing my plate. I sure could use some coffee, though."

"She'll be here in a minute and we'll order a carafe."

Her mother nods and they wait. Mary Alice unwraps the silverware and moves it to the side of her place setting. The butter knife is smooth stainless steel. The weight of it feels good in her hand. She holds it and runs her thumb over the handle. People crowd around the breakfast bar. Most have a dazed look, their hair slightly askew. Shorts and T-shirts. The Sunday morning crowd, just out of bed and ready for food. The church crowd will be in later. Neatly dressed. Wide awake.

"Mouse, I've been thinking. I want you to take care of my things.

I've talked to your sisters and made a list of who gets what."

Mary Alice drums the blade of the knife against the table. "When did you talk to them?"

"I talked to them a couple months ago. Asked them if there was anything of mine they wanted because I wanted to get my affairs in order. I shouldn't have waited this long."

The waitress is at the next table. A family of three. The child is in a high chair. They were ahead of Mary Alice and her mother on the list to be seated. She will be coming to them next. Mary Alice watches the waitress take her book out of her brown apron pocket and smooth the pages back. She cannot look at her mother.

"You never mentioned anything to me."

"I know. But I see you all the time and I have some things I want you to have. I wanted to be fair, so I asked them if there was anything they wanted in particular. Since you're my executor, you'll have to take care of it."

Mary Alice looks at the people filing past the breakfast bar. Some put little piles of rubbery eggs on their dishes and then one or two pieces of meat. Others pile toast, potatoes, bacon, sausage, fruit, whatever they can stuff on the plate. Her mother is waiting. Mary Alice's throat feels stiff as if she can't clear it. She looks down at the table and starts rolling the corner of her place mat.

"Well?"

"Mom, you know I hate to talk about this. It makes me feel awful. There's nothing that'll make it any easier. I'll just leave it to you, okay? Whatever you want."

"It's not practical, Mouse. Ya know we're gonna have to deal with this. I don't want to wait until the last minute."

Reaching across the table, Mary Alice takes her mother's hand and holds it. It is cold and light, so insubstantial in weight that it might be made of the air. She gives it a light squeeze and then withdraws her hand to play with the corners of her mat. The edges curl and fray, but she continues to roll the paper back and forth until the waitress approaches.

"Good morning, ladies. Sorry for the wait. We're a little short-handed this morning. Ready to order?"

Folding her hands on her lap, elbows resting on her chair, her mother shakes her head.

"Just coffee for me."

"Mom, that's not enough. I brought you out for a treat. Try and eat, okay?"

Her mother frowns and looks toward the window. Mary Alice can see her reflection. Her mother is angry and she has her lower lip pushed out like a child's. Mary Alice sighs. Her mother doesn't turn.

"She'll have the Eye-opener, over easy, with wheat toast and I'll have the Sunrise Special, over easy with wheat toast as well. And we'll just take a carafe of decaf and some cream and sweetener, please. Oh, and an orange juice."

Mary Alice waits for the waitress to finish scribbling the order. As the woman sticks her booklet back into her apron and gathers the menu, Mary Alice glances at her mother's reflection again. This time it looks sad, a ghost hovering on the outside wishing to come in. Mary Alice waits, not saying a word. Her mother just needs time. Picking up the knife, she rubs her finger over its smooth surface and looks around the room. The soft ring of dishes and silverware create a pleasant backdrop. The waitress brings the coffee and Mary Alice wraps her hands around the hot cup, letting the heat seep into her fingers. Like her mother's, her hands are always cold.

"Mom, what would you say if I went away for a weekend next month?"

She isn't sure her mother has heard her. Still staring out the window, her mother seems as if she won't answer. Her voice is low and husky.

"And who'll help me, if I need it? One of your sisters?"

"Maybe. I'll have to ask them and if they can't, maybe Eleanor's daughter, Sherry, can help out. You know she offered the last time I saw her at the store."

Her mother turns and looks at her for one long moment. Mary Alice notices that the blue of her eyes is cloudy. When did this happen? When did her mother lose that clear-eyed look of strength? Her mother makes a business of stirring her coffee and tasting it. She puts the cup down softly, slowly and then says, "Where are you planning to go?"

Mary Alice shrugs and sips at her own coffee. It is already luke warm. Restaurant coffee seems never to stay warm. A family comes to sit behind their table. Mary Alice's back is to them but she can feel them as some of the members remove their coats and pull out their chairs. She can feel them nudge her with their hands on the backs of their chairs as they sit down.

"Just thought I'd get away for a bit."

Her mother nods and adjusts her glasses.

"You know, Mouse. I'm not so sure Sherry should be the one to take care of me."

"Why not?"

"Her mother, bless her soul, told me that she's moved in with another woman."

"Sherry's mother?"

"No, Sherry. And I don't know what I think about it."

Her mother shakes her head and makes a little tsk, tsk sound. The waitress appears with their order. Mary Alice waits until she finishes. Her mother is still shaking her head as she puts pepper on her eggs.

"You know, Mom, it could be much worse."

"How can it be worse? It goes against everything I've ever been taught or taught you."

Breaking the egg with the tines of her fork, Mary Alice smiles. The church crowd is starting to come in. The diners are now dressed in suit pants, ties and dresses. They are more reserved than the earlier crowd.

"Sherry could be with a guy who beats the daylight out of her, or comes home drunk all the time. At least she's happy. Or she seems so, whenever I talk to her."

Her mother stops and stares at her. Mary Alice can tell she is remembering Jerry. She has that faint look of distaste. Then she gets back to eating her eggs and toast.

"Suppose you're right. Isn't any of my business, anyhow. She's always been a nice gal to me. Go away with you, then. You don't have to worry about me. I'll get along just fine."

Her mother's hands shake a little as she guides her fork to her mouth. Mary Alice realizes that her mother is not trying to make her feel guilty. It is the fear talking. It is only the fear. Looking out into the sharp sunlight, Mary Alice notices that the parking lot of the tire store is deserted. Cars circle outside looking for a place to park at the restaurant. She looks back at her mother, hunched over in her wheelchair, small and thin. She needs to hug her mother close to her, to hold her. She doesn't move. She feels heavy and made of wood. It is the fear. It is the fear that keeps either one of them from moving, from going anywhere.

It is late afternoon. Mary Alice watches the street from her mother's living room window. Her mother is taking a nap; the trip to breakfast and shopping exhausted her. Two blond children are covered in dust from the roadside where they have been building streets for their minicars. They stand in the gravel paths, screaming. Mary Alice can't make out the faces. Only the difference in size. The little child has a high voice. The word *mom* is barely recognizable in the chilling air. The big one will not let the younger child have any of the cars. As she leans forward, Mary Alice sees her breath against the glass. The little one reaches for the toys and the larger slaps him across the face. Mary Alice stands, something in her swelling and breaking as the crying grows louder. She is unable to move but wonders at the mother. Letting her kids go at it like that. The big one gives the little guy a shove and tosses the toys out into the street. The little one runs up the yard and onto the porch while his larger brother stands at attention. He turns and goes out into the street to fetch the cars. He moves in slow motion, head slightly lowered. Shuffling his feet, he plows through the gravel lanes they worked to build. He inches to the porch. Soon he is lost to the shadows. Swallowed into the house.

Her stomach burns. She can feel it at the base of her throat, like a fist pushing upward. She looks down at her hands holding the Post-its. They are becoming crooked at the tips of her fingers. Just the slightest bit. It is the beginning, her body changing like a river, carving new directions, carrying her downstream. The yellow squares of paper she holds remain blank. Her mother wants her to label, but she can't move. She will wait for her mother to wake.

She looks around the room, dark in the early evening. The images are not sharp. They are hard to hold onto. Her father reclines in his chair, sleeping in front of westerns, his hands lightly coated with lime from cement. Her mother in the kitchen, the radio droning the news while she ekes out dinner. Her sisters bang on the bathroom door fighting over whose turn.

It was his place. The television his pride and joy. His smell is gone, even from his chair. She walks to it and runs her hands along the worn vinyl surface. The green is lighter where he rested his arms and his head. She misses him. She can't remember his face. She closes her eyes and can see his form, his hair, but not his face. She never thought she would be here looking back, searching for him. There is the sound of his voice and of his breathing in the night as he slept in the chair, but she cannot see. Looking around the room, she finds there aren't any pictures. Nothing to mark that he was even here.

She eases herself into the worn recliner, takes the pen from her pocket and writes her name. Bold black against the yellow. She sticks the paper to the back of the chair, then sits and rocks, listening to the creak of the springs. The paper and pen drop to the carpet. She longs for the past even though she knows she would not go back. She looks down at the streaks of blue in her legs and wonders how this happened, how she came to sit in an empty room, how people she loved became images she tries to grasp while aging.

A dog barks outside and someone shouts. There is a big to-do out on the street, but she is too tired to go to the window and look. The arms of the chair are smooth and cold. She runs her hands over them, drawing invisible circles. Her mother is so quiet tonight. Mary Alice resists the urge to check on her. Just like when the kids were little. She is only sleeping.

Mary Alice looks around the room in the half-light. Colors are still visible, muted. She does not want to catalog. Picking out items makes her feel like a hyena, circling the remains of a majestic animal. There is an organ in the corner and a clock. Her sisters will want these. But Mary Alice wants nothing except the little things, the things that have the surfaces worn by use, like the silver tin her mother used for buttons. Mary Alice rises and crosses to the mantel. Even in the gloom, the wood is smooth and warm. The tin is heavy with buttons. It rattles as she moves it, her fingers fumbling with the knob on the lid. Buttons, her mother's little treasures, colored like pills, saved for the day when they might be needed. So many buttons. No one has needed any for a long time. This is something Mary Alice will put her name to. Something that is her mother. Across the mantel are small silver animals. Something about them has always fascinated her mother and the children in her life. Tiny faces, heavy metal fur. A story for each to be told at night or nap time. It is hard to swallow.

Mary Alice takes a deep breath and moves away. She goes to the window and looks out at the street. It is quiet now. An occasional car passes. No one else. The clock behind her rings, in deep tones, churchlike. Time for her to fix dinner and wake her mother. Suddenly, she wants very much to see her, talk to her. She turns from the window and takes a look around the dimming room. The yellow square is just visible on the back of her father's chair. She doesn't know how to get through this.

She makes herself walk away and into the kitchen. She will keep herself busy. She reaches down and pulls the frying pan out of the cabinet. There is a slight ring as she lifts the lid. A drop falls into the middle of the pan and spreads, little hairlike projections radiating outward. She looks and then finds another. Wiping at her eyes, she swallows and sniffs. Turning, she crosses to the refrigerator and opens it. Milk, eggs, sausage, ham, leftover pie. It doesn't matter what she cooks, her mother won't eat it anyway. She grabs the milk. Cold and heavy. She selects the eggs and sausage, and gets a bowl out of the cabinet. She turns the pan on low to preheat and begins to cut the sausage into patties. The routine calms her.

Jane Morrel

───◆───

Alberta Lived To Be Ninety-Three

Alberta, looking these of your years, all days
At a water oak, from your chair.

Tell us, Alberta, we said,
Were you in love, tell us
About your children, your life, your politics?
About, tell us,
When you were, yes, a little girl?

Acorn dishes, I liked the most, I loved them
When I was a little girl
A lamb ate my mother's cherry pie
On a windowsill —
She set it there to cool. Why don't we go
Where Mother is, out under the sycamore tree?
We can make dishes from acorns — set places for
Hollis and Barnet. Set one for Mary, Jo.

Love — love — there was Barnet — his beautiful horse,
Sherry, that Barnet drove, shiny as my silk dress
Yes, love? — Hollis walked with me
Three years. We did not even kiss.
Barnet said let us get married — he flicked his whip
It was a new whip. Sherry was almost human —
I looked in the eye of the beast. He laughed,
He laughed at me, it seems to me. And he said, yes, yes —
Barnet gave Sherry to me.
Hollis is coming, tonight, I think — tell me
How do I look? He likes my hair this way.

Yes, Barnet and I were married forty years —
Barnet is currying Sherry down at the stables — would
Someone call him for me?
I haven't seen him all day. Don't tell him
I told you — but I thought
I thought, I heard Alberta cry.
My children? There must have been three
Some of the others died when they were born
It appears to me.

I remember there was a letter — Toby was killed
In the Argonne. Yes, now I'm sure
That Barnet and I were with him. Toby was killed
    all right,
In some war. Why are you crying? Toby was born
Last night and I am so happy. So strong, so much hair
More than the others had. I remember, well,
There was a girl called Alberta, there.

Politics? Barnet and I used to vote.
I was walking down the river road —
Someone, I remember, said to me
Our President is dead. His name? His name?
Republican or Democrat? I don't know. But
A brown-looking bird, upon a post, I never did forget
And Alberta was with me there.

Oh Alberta, Alberta, sitting there
Looking these of your years, all days
At a water oak, from your chair.

Celia Wesle

◆

Poems

From the Train Window

The goldenrod
Wraps its stalks and plumes
Around scattered
Pipes and boards

Over the shorter
Sweet William,
Thrusting here and there
Between the grasses.

Queen Anne's lace
Has a space or two
To complete
The pattern of
Yellow, lavender and cream
Among the green
To keep
The scream of trash
Strewn about
Muted in the
September sunshine,
Near the railroad tracks
At the backs
Of the houses.

The Painting

Madam X
has a wide V
at the top
in the front
of her dress.

John Singer
Sargent sang
her splendor.
Madam X,
dignified,
is looking away
while showing
clearly
her lovely profile,
her unjeweled ear,
neck and shoulders,
her pale lavender skin.

How lightly
she leans
on her fingers
touching the small table,
her right hip
curved outward
as her left leg
takes the weight —
all under
a long black gown.

But first
when we look,
we see
the V.

Walk to School

She carefully sets
the long, bright yellow
loosely knit scarf
to look tossed
around her waving
yellow hair,
blue eyes bright.

Last year she
bundled as usual
against the Wisconsin cold
with lined hood
over wool cap,
heavy mittens, thick boots,
books hugged to her chest.
Nature had first
loosed the lining
of her womb
four years ago,
but now she blooms.

She's fifteen.
Her body glows,
her face sparkles,
she so warms
the atmosphere
around her head
that those yellow
strands of yarn,
one square inch apart,
catch and hold
against the snowflakes
a magic winter heat,
and she floats cozy
down the street
and feels pleased and pretty.

Lovely

Dimple and pretty teeth,
genteel of manner
but dependable
and strong, slim,
good cook and seamstress,
ideal old-fashioned wife
(wonderful present day person).
She would spontaneously
harmonize to his tenor
as they played zither
and guitar together.

My father adored her long
chestnut-brown braids,
brushed and rebraided,
wound after sleep
against the back of her head.
At his fervent request
she avoided the flapper cuts.
I remember the narrow
black velvet ribbon
tied around it daily
when I was little.
I would watch its dark
fuzzy texture bound by
tiny shiny satin edges
as her head moved.

They danced beautifully,
She was fun, wrote
amusing verses my sister and I
would recite for parties.
She liked the joyfulness
of religion and
depended on meditative prayers.
She saw my dad
as her handsome, gifted prince.

I asked her once
if Papa ever expressed
a desire to return to Germany.
She reflected a minute
then smiled and said,
*"Nein, nie. Er wollte immer
sein wo ich bin."*
No never. He always wanted to be
where I am.

From the Porch Swing

Break off the branch,
saw it away.
What does the
pussy willow deva say:

"No matter it is dead —
no life for leaves,
it's a blue jay's perch,
swings in the breeze.

Your Germanic correctness
is no help now,
flow with what is
like the bird on the bough."

The Decades

If the lace on the camisole
has loosened and shredded a bit,
do you in '70s style
discard, make room for new?

Or, do you, in '30s style
slip on your silver thimble,
admire the shallow metal scrollwork
of plant forms circling
its dimpled top,
find cream-colored thread,
a fine but big-eyed embroidery needle,
proceed to preserve in '90s
ecologically correct
recycling style,
and think as you stitch
about its effect
under your suits
below your neck
over your bosom?

I Hear Her

Clickity click
Like high heels
Coming across
The linoleum floor.
It's not
A short-stepping
Young lady
But an old dog,
With nails rather long,
Come to find crumbs
Under the kitchen table.

Spiritual Rejuvenation

Mother will be
Ninety next month.
Her house is
Suddenly so shiny.
She seems to have forgotten
Her aching hip and back.
She touches her cheek
With a tender smile.
The new young priest
Came to visit:

He stayed two hours.
He picked up
Her wedding picture
Again and again —
Seeing the beautiful
Regal lady
In '20s simple lace
Next to the
Handsome tall blond
Holding his top hat.

The former parish priest is gone.
"What do I need
With a bitter old man?"
She says to me,
Her fingertips on her cheek
Where her new visitor kissed her,
Having promised to
Lead the rosary
At the funeral home
When the time comes
To maintain her honor
With her churchy relatives.

Weaving

I. The weaver leans forward,
shoots the shuttle of woof
between the two warp rows,
arms stretch
for the catch and return.
She uses her feet
like an organist
on the pedals below.
The rhythms repeat
as if a litany or song.
Muscles in her middle
control in all directions.

II. Cloth World has a
universe of choices:
soft and stiff fabrics,
wide or skinny laces,
ribbons, all sizes of
scissors and buttons.
I ask the saleslady, "Where
do you keep the darning cotton?"
"Darning cotton?" she asks, puzzled.
I say, "Yes, thread to darn socks."
She shakes her head.
"We wouldn't have anything like that."

III. Sister Honora, sewing class,
how to weave a cross.
Then in and out,
back and forth
to darn stockings.
A skill I perfected.
I feel connected
with my great, great grandmothers
who lived in German houses
that are still standing,
hinged at one corner
to allow large looms
to be moved in and out.

IV. Beauty of vision:
I watch the exact and
growing pattern.
Dance of motion.
It is in my fingers.
I choose not to
give up these pleasures:
there are holes to be filled!
My friend has punctured
two new pairs of socks.
I buy light gray embroidery
thread, instead.
My weaving will be on view
from his open-toed Birkenstocks.

The Bath

A pale warm skin sack,
more beautiful than a
Hallmark gift bag
(has curving contours),
holds her
valuable innards.
She lowers it gently
into blossom fallout,
daughter having moved
the green geranium boxes
next to the tub onto the
blue bathroom window sills.

She floats with the
soft salmon, red,
pink petal disks —
a Hawaiian forest pool.
The Dove-scented washcloth
strokes her surface,
grown long ago
from ectomorph cells
like her ears and brain,
and she hears and thinks
freshly with sensitized skin.

Sandra Olivetti Martin

◆

A Hero Among Women

Rosie lived in the Golden Age.

In those charmed years, women — who were all beautiful — were lovers and mothers and poets and the best of friends. For fun, they'd lie in the summer sun baking and telling each other stories about how, someday soon, their ships would come in. Even if, right now, those ships might be delayed, banked offshore or boarded by pirates. Alone, they told the best stories of all: poems and bittersweet stories or pictures and paintings that soon they'd get together to share with their friends.

If no matter how hard they worked, ends didn't quite meet, or if by day they worked in the sterile halls of State or County Govmint — so what? In those charmed years, all the women were heroes and Rosie was a hero among women. Rosie, we called her for short and sweet, but her name, Rosemary, is for remembrance.

Rosie could, all her life, have stayed anonymous in the basement of Illinois National Bank in a decaying downtown. After all, she was just a Springfield girl who lived in the projects, her front door facing poor whites and her back door facing poor blacks. She was half Jewish and half Gentile, with a mother "working hard to make ends meet" and no visible father. "I don't remember much about Dad," Rosie wrote in her stories, *Christmas Cake* and *Ella*. "Mom said he was a good man, but he lived too far away to come see us. Joe said he was a rat, and he was glad Dad left. Alana kept a picture of him on her dresser, but she kept her bedroom door locked so Grandma wouldn't destroy it. Grandma said Dad was a bum . . . "

Could Rosie ever have been "just" anything? What would you have thought if you'd seen her dancing lunch hours away in the gym at Lanphier High to scratchy fifties records? Could you have known that, at home, Rosie's mother was going downhill fast on her way to the State Hospital? Her friend Polly Poskin knew: "One of the organizing principles of Rosie's life was that she never wanted to have happen to her what had happened to her mother: the breakdowns. Rosie had taken responsibility for hospitalizing and caring for her mother. She never wanted that to happen to her or to her children."

Before the Golden Age when the women got to be heroes, girls hoped to marry their future. The love of the right kind of man could make you respectable, even if you had dark secrets. Like not knowing who your father was. Like knowing what your mother was capable of, as Rosie did in her story, *Mom*, the tale of a mother who ran away to Memphis to be with Elvis.

Rosie, the teenage bank clerk, married a bank officer. She had two kids and another dose of tragedy, as she related in "Bad Blood," a poem she wrote in 1993: "He is your son, your youngest child, born red but turns chalk-white-blue. You take him to six doctors in six weeks. A doctor orders a blood count and sends him to the hospital for a transfusion. 'His hemoglobin dropped. We don't know why. We're lucky he's alive. One more week and he would have been dead.' He is pink but not whole. At twenty-three, he can't read. You find out he has extra pieces on six pairs of chromosomes. You puzzle over the connections."

Was this the Rosie who wrote, "I don't feel like falling apart over death. I fall apart over life"? Then, if ever, she might have believed the plans for her ship were lost in the building yard.

Not even those "crazy desperate times" could put Rosie down, Donna Rich-Murdock remembers: "We met when we both showed up, uncomfortably pregnant, at a bridge club where we'd been invited by a mutual friend. The year was 1968. Neither of us was feeling in blossom the way pregnant women are supposed to. Rosie started complaining and wisecracking and we got to laughing and hit it off. It's always been that way with Rosie. People accepted her because secretly they were feeling the same thing but she's saying it in that witty intelligent way of hers that makes everything exact."

From the bud, the rose opens. The force is in the flower. In a Golden Age, who knows what wonder may blossom?

In 1970, when Rosie was bursting with the urgency of twenty-six years of life, the Lords of the Prairie said, "Let there be levity," and Sangamon State University grew in the cornfields. When SSU opened its downtown campus, Rosie went back to school — just around the corner from work. Ideas were hopping like popcorn.

Judy Everson sees her still: "Rose . . . her large dark eyes, her marvelously innovative manner of dressing, her exuberance for life.

Like so many students, she was not really certain of herself, wondering what she would become. She was a sponge in my classes like 'Images of Women in Literature,' soaking in so much while finding her own voice. She's the sort of student SSU was set up to help blossom. And she did."

In the early seventies, ideas were heady, arousing. (Don't you remember Brainchild founder Peg Knoepfle writing: "My friends are high-strung fillies, oversexed from the neck up"?) People were looking at each other, giving each other the eye, and telling their stories. Heads opened eyes opened mouths opened doors — and people walked through.

Donna: "Our next step was having the strength to get out . . . going back to school when husbands didn't want us to. Afterwards we'd go to the Curve Inn to talk, do our homework, read Shakespeare out loud. Here we were, these old women with kids going back to school — taking every class Mike Lennon taught — and studying nothing we'd make a living out of."

That's the Rosie Polly first knew: "When I met Rosie, she was recently divorced and had moved into a top floor apartment on Park Street with her two little darling children, Stacia and Alan. She was always struggling: child care, her job, working on a degree at SSU."

Like the Old Woman Who Lived in the Shoe, the women had too many children, for these were the mothers of Cookie Monster. The babies: Alan, Jessica, Joshua, Nat, Shannon, Zoe. The kids: Stacie, Rolf, Bridget, Natasha, Stefan. The big kids: Claudia, Lex. We bonded together in our cooperative child-care center to buy ourselves affordable freedom to study, to work, and to soar. Here the mothers became sisters, twinned and twined by their parallel stories, and all the children whose diapers we changed became our godchildren. Of all the sisters, Rosie's times were the hardest. While other children were naughty, coquettish or Houdini-like, Alan was sweet and slow. Other children might get scarlet fever; Alan got meningitis.

Don't shed too many a tear over those hard times. A job was work and children were a struggle, but in life's important aspects, our hero Rosie and her friends had learned to stop struggling. Ours was a Golden Age and we were flowing with the river. Lives had as many dimensions as the diamonds that used to be girls' best friends — and we had to have them all at once: children, independence, education, art, freedom, love.

That's what Rosie wrote about in her novel, *Fifth Position*, according to her sister in literature Peg Knoepfle: "It's about moving from being a housewife in a bad marriage to being a woman raising two children — one needing special care — trying to get an education — all while learning to do ballet's fifth position at Katherine

Dunham's East St. Louis dance school." Sex was a hot one of those dimensions. That aspect of self, strictly forbidden to girls growing up in the fifties, was a rite of passage for women blossoming in the seventies. So we all laugh, blushingly, as we remember the other thing *Fifth Position's* heroine is trying to learn: to do oral sex.

In the late seventies, Peg heard Rosie read that story at the old Crows Mills School. She remembers "a mixed audience, and sitting right in front of the speaker's stand were four young women, clerical workers and aides, women in bureaucracy enjoying their evening drink after putting in their time at Lincoln Land or Sangamon State. They were pretty bored until Rosie started to read. At the first indication of what it was about, they sat up with their eyes wide. By the end of the selection they were standing and cheering — as was everybody else in the room. Toni Morrison wanted to publish that novel. I think she was outmaneuvered by the conservatism of the early eighties. I still think it's a major novel of the 1970s."

Stepping out on our own was a compulsory part of the program: you had to step so far out you might spin right off into space. Donna was Rosie's first stepping-out partner: "When I got divorced, I took the money I got from my ring and my oven and hitchhiked with Rosie to San Francisco. We didn't know what we'd do or where we'd stay; we just ended up there, climbing and almost dying on the cliffs. We were hitching that day with two guys and their blind dog named Rosie. What we wanted to do that day was hike and see sights, and they took us on a beautiful trail that descended into a deep ocean gully. We were swimming and having a beautiful time, when the tide came in. Our only escape was to climb up that cliff. With the steeply flat surface and the waves roaring below, we thought we were going to die full of fear and thinking of our kids back in Illinois. Now Rosie's never been much of an athlete, but since that blind dog was making it up, Rosie said she could. Up at the top, we'd survived and the sun was shining. We thought we were going to die together and we've survived together. We've had a lot of altered states, but that's one of the most amazing."

We were liberated, but we hadn't forgotten the comforts of home. After all, good girls that we were, we'd played our best at every role. We'd learned to be wives; now we turned our wifely attentions to people who'd appreciate them: ourselves, our friends, our children and our lovers.

Rosie's apartments, beginning with Park Street, were a world away from the shabby married apartment above the drugstore, as seen in her prize-winning story "Socks and Earrings" by her alter ego Ellen: "How awful. It was little and dark. And all those steps. She remembers lugging groceries and laundry up them. Outside staircase. Aqua swirled carpet. She hated it. Small rooms. No window in the bedroom."

At Rosie's, women reveled in the apotheosis of girlhood dreams and everybody had a good time. Lynda Dautenhahn had a good time: "On Park Street, Rosie had wonderful white furniture and this huge green-striped couch left over from her marriage. We spent many hours talking on it." Diana Pippi had a good time: "We'd sit on each end of her big green couch, eating chips and dip and gossiping. We'd talk about our ships coming in." Now they were banked offshore or pirated, but they were certain to come in sometime. The kids might be watching TV and there'd be children's books around. When the women, advised by St. Paul, gave up the things of a child, life had turned very dull. Rediscovered, silly pleasures were delicious.

As mothers recreating themselves while raising their children, the women were fun. Weaned on independence bought through shared responsibility, most of our little Cookie Monsters grew up independent, smart, responsible and good-looking, like Stacia. Alan is the one who became special.

Polly knew their mother-son relationship inside out: "Rosie was Alan's connection, the bridge from his limited world to our bigger one. She allowed him freedom of expression and gave him freedom from prejudice. She helped him develop his taste. Alan's knowledge of reggae and movies and counterculture have given him awareness and sophisticated social skills, far beyond what you'd expect in a person of his IQ. This kid, who can't read, reads reggae magazines from cover to cover; he's quite a movie analyst. I learned to know mentally retarded people through Rosie and how to accept what they teach us."

Motherhood reconciled the women even to Springfield. Sure, they wanted to get out. In the golden days, woman after woman tried her wings — usually turning them westward. California didn't work out for Rosie any better than for most of the women. Ellen of "Socks and Earrings" reflects on one species of the women's disappointments: "She was stuck in San Jose living in a rented house in the suburbs where the neighbors didn't speak to her because they thought she was poor white trash. . . . After six months, Ellen and her daughter left. Came home. To the prairie, where the streets were narrow and the sky was plentiful. . . . Ellen stayed with her friend, Star, who was earthy and natural. She taught Ellen how to take care of plants and kids, how to be mellow without drugs, and how to be nice."

Rosie had another reason to stay home: Alan. Polly Poskin: "One of Rosie's deep dilemmas was how to realize what she wanted for herself while being Alan's channel to realize himself. She thought to become what she wanted to be, she'd have to leave Springfield. But she could never leave her son."

Subtly, without our much noticing, we got competent. We made homes. In 1979 or 1980, Rosie set up housekeeping with Polly and Pippi on Washington Street. Three years later, Rosie and Stacia migrated to 117 South Grand Avenue West, the three-story, six-flat brick building with its two outdoor plaster goddesses.

To support our children and ourselves, we got jobs. At first, that seemed to mean going to work for the Springfield establishment: state, city or university. City Water, Light and Power liked Rosie's snappy style and new degree. As public information officer, she wrote their newsletter and gave tours at the city power plant. For the State of Illinois, Rosie worked at Department of Personnel, traveling the state doing training. She wowed people with her skill and style — and kept wowing people as a free-lance consultant. Rosie, like her alter ego Ellen in "Triple Word Sting," got good at being a management consultant, "telling people what to do and looking for results."

Changing — and disillusioning — politics ended both jobs. Rosie faced a difficult period of unemployment, searching for what she wanted to do. She'd never work for government again, she swore.

The women had become very competent. No longer cogs in somebody else's — city or state or university father's — machine, they created their own machines to do the work men left undone. Through direct action, organization, and policy, they fought violence and sexual assault. Rosie went to work with friends for a cause she could believe in: the Illinois Coalition Against Sexual Assault. Donna remembers those times — when Rosie was working part-time for ICASA and doing her own workshops on stress management and report writing — as "the best time, when she was the happiest." But Rosie thought she'd do better on her own, supporting herself with her consulting business, teaching and writing.

Illinois then went into its lingering depression, and trainers without political connection were dropped. From that time on, Rosie was struggling financially. She tried writing resumes for hire. She tried what Peg calls "this John Hancock thing, Rosie and this bunch of guys obsessed with money, who fell in love with her." Rosie had some successes selling insurance. She put together a quarter of a million dollar life-insurance policy to benefit her kids, joking, "I wish I could get some of that money alive."

But mostly, selling insurance was awful. Ginny Lee, another "free spirit out of work and looking for possibilities to make money," minces no words about that: "We became very good friends because it's so awful. I can't imagine anything worse than life insurance because people hate insurance salespeople — even when you're nice to them. It's the cold, cruel world. So Rosie and I became very close. We called ourselves the 'cold-calling cowgirls.'"

At her typewriter, Rosie came in from the cold. Her stories and poems elevated the daily arts to sacred rituals and helped take the sting out of life's thorny problems — like how to live with cars and kids and bad haircuts and how to survive your lover. Peg Knoepfle: "The man in her life for close to twenty years was the poet Ricardo Amézquita. They had a wonderful relationship made up by the two of them. During one period when they were not seeing each other, at Brainchild we'd get a new story each month about meeting this wonderful dark-haired and dark-eyed Hispanic man. That's how we always knew they'd get back together."

As for so many women in Springfield, Brainchild — the women's writing collective — was Rosie's lifeline. Peg, Brainchild's godmother: "After poetry books 3 and 4, Brainchild had fallen through the cracks. Rosie pulled it out. In the late 1970s, Rosie got in touch with me, determined it should keep going. For a while there, Brainchild was held up by the thread of Rosie and I reading to one another. It meant a whole lot to me, working at my first job, feeling a total failure and alienated from everybody I knew. Rosie plucked me out of that. Then old Brainchildren Pat Hilton and Katherine Lawson came back. Then Jessica Billings, Cheryl Frank and then more collected. Rosie made it possible to say Brainchild was continuous."

"Brainchild is a place to go, a place to be understood and misunderstood," Rosie said when the group was compiling its sixth anthology. "It's a circle that changes and remains the same. The poems, the prose, the words keep us alive, make us probe our own demons, find them and shake them. Honesty. Understanding. Sisterhood. The power of stories. A respite from those who think the conscious world is the only reality. A place where reality and fantasy commingle like old friends."

One of Brainchild's gifts was to make each sister's musings public and real, transforming them into literature. In readings and anthologies, Brainchild extended the charmed circle created by Rosie's writings, poems and — with increasing dominance, stories. The circle extended further and further. In 1986, Rosie won Lincoln Library's coveted Writer of the Year award for her story "Socks and Earrings." To her delight, she was selected to be a fellow at the prestigious Helene Wurlitzer Foundation in Taos. That she was still waiting for her time there to come when death called early was, she told many friends, her only regret.

Rosie told her stories in *Illinois Times* as well. Usually she wrote about other people's quest for art; always, she was part of her stories. To salve their wounds, Rosie and Ginny Lee collaborated on writing and photographing for *Illinois Times*. Stories on Arlin of Arlin's Cafe. Mauri Formigoni and David Hammons and their art. "Rosie would talk with the person so I could photograph them at ease," said Ginny.

Jim Huston saw the difference Rosie made: "Rosie didn't make much money off her writing but it made great joy, giving an incredible amount to the whole city of Springfield."

When Rosie had written, she came out to play with her friends.

You know Rosie's friendship. You've played all the wonderful games with Rosie. You've shared champagne out of plastic glasses so you could afford to throw brunches. You've breakfasted and bicycled with her through Springfield. You've caught her in the mulberry bush with her lips purple and mouth full of sweet. You've gotten up early with her to pick strawberries in the dew. You've climbed the cherry tree with her, made Valentine's cards and played Scrabble with her, drunk her Christmas killer punch. Certainly you've laughed with her: laughed, laughed, laughed until both your stomachs hurt.

Pippi laughed with Rosie: "We wanted to go to Oregon and no money. My mother said it was begging, but we didn't care. We decided to give something for your money. We had our fund-raiser. I had made a few Freudian slips, the sort you wear under dresses, with a safety pin attached to each slip. To one of them, Rosie pinned her letter from Toni Morrison, a nice, handwritten letter. She called it 'Rejection Slip on Freudian Slip.' I think she sold the actual letter. We made masks of people's faces with plaster of paris and soap. You could have your picture taken with my picture of Andy Warhol. We had a Jesse Helms dart board on the back porch. Singer Linda Schneider from ICASA and Jim the organist put out a hat. Rosie sold tapes of her work. We made maybe $800 — maybe I'm exaggerating a few hundred — but enough to go out to Oregon for a week, where we read and ate and walked on the beach."

"Generosity" touches every tongue when thoughts turn to Rosie. Part of her generosity was to make room for every comer in art's circle. In 1989, Rosie sold her old buddy Mike Lennon, then head of Public Affairs for SSU, on the idea of an access-channel TV show, *Works in Progress*. Peg Knoepfle became Rosie's on-air partner: "When we walked in for our first show, I was broke from paying for kids in college, so I lacked quite a few teeth, which you saw if I smiled too widely. Rosie was letting her dye job grow out and had a skunk streak. But we had great fun and a great audience. State workers, writers, truck drivers. When Rosie would go to the post office, clerks would all say, 'Hey, I saw you!'"

Yes, says Lynda Dautenhahn, Rosie was generous: "Rosie has always extended herself to other people, lots of different kinds of people. Without the direct closeness of a family, it always seemed like she was creating a very large family."

That's us.

When the awful news came — the devouring, voracious cancer — Rosie's family surrounded her with love, piling gifts around her bed. Donna had "never seen anything like this before. These beautiful women are always here, patting, kissing, reading, encouraging, asking what she needs. Everyone is giving something."

The love Rosie had sent into the world rolled back in waves. "I knew Milli liked me," Rosie told Janice DiGirolamo at Polly's birthday party, "but I never knew how much she loved me." Now she knew. Milli had evolved from pal and counselor to one of the team of omnipresent companions and nurses. First singly, then, when moving became too hard, in pairs, Polly, Pippi, Carol, Milli and how many others tended Rosie's body and comforted her soul.

Rosie's sisters — Jo-Anne D'Auria from Chicago and Judie Bakke from Texas, each one stealing time from death — gathered round her. Stacia led a legion of twenty-five-year-olds — among them Bridget Murdock, her best friend since Cookie Monster — to Rosie's bed, as if their youth would rekindle her life. Ricardo Amézquita wrote her a poem and brought her an angel scarf to go at her bedside. Sandra Bartholemy, a Cookie Monster sister, drove from Michigan through a snowstorm to say good-bye. Nancy Imhoff massaged Rosie's aching body. Lynda Dautenhahn helped Rosie write her thank-you notes to Rosie Fund contributors. From *Illinois Times*, Bill Furry serenaded Rosie. All of her friends cooked — all of them fretting, like Janice DiGirolamo, over what might tempt Rosie's appetite back or calm her nasty nausea. Like Janice — who froze her meals in individual portions in little bread pans labeled with contents and cooking directions — everyone took such special care.

Rosie's room was full of flowers and she had a basket of cards a mile deep . . . and all those people held her in their hearts. Their love was background music for Rosie's dying. Rosie was ready, she told me. In those last weeks, Rosie prepared herself well. She re-embraced Judaism, discussing, debating, mingling its longing of life's meaning with her own short, sharp insight until, at her funeral, Rabbi Barry Marks of Temple Israel could speak of her from the confidence of friendship. "He had her to a tee," said Janice of his eulogy.

Alan's future was Rosie's last achievement. From her deathbed, she advocated for him with Jayne McDonald, a friend whose husband, Jess, headed the Illinois Department of Mental Health and Developmental Disabilities. The next morning, Jess McDonald came himself to Rosie's bedside and held her hand, promising to move Alan into a higher-level home with more opportunity. "This was something she always strove to do in life. Now, in her dying state, she has brought a better life to Alan," said Polly. Now Rosie could give herself to death's journey.

She left us in the last hours of March 1, circled round in love and strength. Stacia, Bridget, Micky and Liesl for youth. Jim, Polly, Pippi, Carol, Milli and Nancy for long times. Nancy: "Before lapsing into a coma, Rosie was in a lot of pain and refused medication. Her pain was like labor, like birthing her own soul to be free."

Marcia Salner and the good women of Temple Israel received Rosie's body to prepare her for her journey. Rosie would be the first person for whom Marcia would do this final kindness, and they had talked long of what would be done. This is how Rosie was washed and dressed for death on March 2, as Janice DiGirolamo recollects Marcia's words to her at Rosie's funeral, March 3: "They began with a prayer for doing things right the first time. Then they asked forgiveness from Rosie just in case they didn't handle her as she would have wanted. Rosie's face was very peaceful, her eyes closed, her features beautiful and classic. After the ritual washing, they dressed her in ritual clothes that signify everyone's equality at death: linen pants sewn at bottom so her feet didn't stick out, with a tie at her waist just folded under, so in heaven her clothes and all earthly possessions will just drop away; a blouse, little vest, and old-fashioned white linen cap; lace cloths over her bodice and face. Rosie looked very beautiful."

Rosie lies close to her grandmother in the Jewish section of Oak Ridge Cemetery beneath her own angel carved in stone from Pippi's image. Pippi imagines Rosie now, joining a flock of laughing angels: "I hope they dress like the San Francisco Sisters of Perpetual Indulgence and drive red Saab convertibles."

Born August 20, 1944. Gone in her fiftieth year: March 1, 1994. Our times together have been golden, but Rosie has run ahead . . .

Voices
   from the past
      still echo
in the inner catacombs
   like the drone
      of bees
rising and falling
   in the dark
      cavity
of a matriarchal tree
   old
      limbs
         stretched
            wide.

Poem by Pat Martin. Artwork by Kate Kanaley Miller

Vicki Bamman is an adoption counselor for Lutheran Child and Family Services in Springfield, and a juried member of the Prairie Art Alliance. She has been published in *Echo VI*, and has co-authored materials for the Transition Institute, which prepares special education students for jobs.

Becky Bradway, former editor of *Writers' Bar-B-Q*, lives in Bloomington, Illinois. She has published fiction in *Laurel Review, South Carolina Review, Beloit Fiction Journal, Crescent Review, Other Voices, Sojourner, American Fiction, Sequoia, Mississippi Valley Review, The Greensboro Review* and numerous other publications.

ABOUT THE AUTHORS ♦ 195

Rena Brannan, writer/hairdresser, lives with her partner and two children in a small English village two hours outside of London. In the past year, she has written *Pink Ears,* a sitcom; *Obstacle Course,* a play; and *Paper Cuts,* an anthology of short fiction.

Deborah Brothers teaches composition and literature at Lincoln Land College in Springfield, and is a doctoral student in English at Illinois State University. This spring, she won Lincoln Library's Writer of the Year award for nonfiction, and her most recently published work appeared in the April 1997 *English Journal.* She is married, has two children, and can still walk on stilts.

Gael Carnes is currently working on two novels, in between raising KateandMackenzie (all one word, she says). She has won two artist advancement awards from the Springfield Area Arts Council. Her work has appeared in *Alchemist Review*, *Writers' Bar-B-Q, Lunium Wonders, Southern Illinois Accent* and Brainchild anthologies.

Sue Daugherty lives in Danville, Illinois, where she works at home, raising three daughters, writing, baking, painting, gardening "and otherwise making stuff." Her work has appeared in several student publications, and she has been featured on the Springfield public access television show *Works in Progress.*

Roberta DeKay, a Brainchild member in the 1970s, now lives in San Jose, California. Her work has been published in *Illinois Times, Alchemist Review,* and the journal *Reflections.* Five of her poems will appear in *Poetic Medicine: The Healing Art of Poem-Making,* to be published by Jeremy Thatcher/Putnam Co. this fall.

Debi Sue Edmund is a public relations consultant, and is pursuing a master's degree in child, family and community services from the University of Illinois at Springfield. She spent several years as a newspaper and magazine journalist, and has won awards from the Associated Press and the Mississippi Valley Writers Conference.

Tavia Ervin, an assessment coordinator at the University of Illinois at Springfield, is also a student at Bethany Theological Seminary, where she is studying to be a minister for the Church of the Brethren. Her book reviews and essays have appeared in *Illinois Times.*

Photos: Top row, from left, Debby, Becky, Gael. Row 2: Rena, Sue, Tavia. Row 3: Vicki, Debi, Roberta.

Jacqueline Jackson teaches writing and literature at the University of Illinois at Springfield. *The Round Barn,* to be published in 1999, contains stories, oral history, biography, scientific accounts and other material centered around the Wisconsin dairy farm where she grew up. *Stories from the Round Barn,* selections from the larger work, will be published in 1997 by Northwestern University.

Kate Kanaley Miller began writing 25 years ago "to save my life, journaling my way out of a chaos of confusion. I write to make sense of the world, putting into words what impacts my being." She is a former environmental educator recovering from the effects of Lyme disease, remembering the blessings in each day, and Grandmothering. She's working on a chapbook of her writing and artwork and a recording of her cedar flute music.

ABOUT THE AUTHORS ♦ 197

Peg Knoepfle teaches composition at Springfield College, produces the public access TV show *Works in Progress,* volunteers at the Heartland Peace Store, and is a member of the Springfield Solidarity Committee and the Women's International League for Peace and Freedom. She is author of a chapbook, *Sparks from Your Hooves;* editor of the book *After Alinksy: Community Organizing in Illinois;* and has appeared in several Brainchild anthologies.

Bonnie Madison, a second grade teacher in Petersburg, Illinois, has written poetry, short stories and teaching materials. Her work has appeared in *Alchemist Review*, *Rosie: Selected Works by Rosemary Richmond*, previous Brainchild anthologies and an anthology produced by Elderhostel's Iowa Writers Workshop.

Pat Martin, executive secretary in the Office of the Illinois Attorney General, writes poetry and stories "from a distinctly female perspective, focusing on and honoring experiences and feelings that have been ignored or minimized in the testosterone-dominated society of the last two thousand years." She's won several writing awards.

Sandra Martin, a founding member of Brainchild, is now editor-in-chief of the *New Bay Times Weekly,* her family's alternative newspaper in Maryland.

Carol Manley has been published in *Alchemist Review, Illinois Times, Sounds from the Sangamon, Earth's Daughters* and *Lines in the Sand*. She won Lincoln Library's Writer of the Year award in 1995, has been a participant at Ragdale, and has appeared on the public access television show *Works in Progress.*

Martha McGill has been writing for more than four decades. She has appeared in *Alchemist Review,* served as contributing editor on newsletters, and developed training and reference manuals. Her poem *Old Photographs: 1860-1900* was awarded Best of Show in the 1990 On My Own Time competition in Springfield. She is the mother of five, grandmother of eleven and great-grandmother of three.

Linda McElroy writes newsletters, journal articles and speeches for the Illinois State Board of Education. Her stories have been published in *Alchemist Review,* and she has won four awards for her fiction in the annual citywide exhibit On My Own Time.

Photos: Top row, from left, Jackie, Marty, Kate. Row 2: Carol, Linda, Peg. Row 3: Sandra, Pat, Bonnie.

Martha Miller has had four plays produced by Mid-America Playwrights theater, and her short fiction is widely published. In 1995, she won Lincoln Library's Writer of the Year award and the *Illinois Times* reader's poll for the Best Author in Springfield. *Seductions*, her collection of short fiction, will be published in 1998 by New Victoria Press, and she is currently working on a mystery.

Maria Mootry is director of African American Studies and associate professor of English at the University of Illinois at Springfield. She founded The Poetry Factory, a writers' group in Carbondale, Illinois, and co-edited *A Life Distilled*, a collection of critical essays on the writings of Gwendolyn Brooks. Her writing has appeared in *Open Places*, *Full Circle*, *The Otherwise Room* and *Stop the Violence!*

ABOUT THE AUTHORS ♦ 199

Jane Morrel, teacher and poet, was a founding member of Brainchild. Her literary career began in 1942, and her work appeared in numerous publications, including *Colorado Quarterly, Mississippi Valley Review* and the *St. Louis Post-Dispatch*.

Nancy Pistorius has been a teacher, technical writer, news reporter, columnist, editor (of *Spoon River Literary Review*), researcher, editorial assistant, public relations writer and feature writer. Her work has appeared in more than sixty publications, including *The New Kent Quarterly, Cosmopolitan* and *Woman's Day*.

Rosemary Richmond was co-host of the public access television show *Works in Progress*. Her work appeared in *Alchemist Review, Two Way Mirrors, XX Chromosome Chronicle* and *Illinois Times*. A Lincoln Library Writer of the Year, she nurtured and encouraged numerous writers and authors over the years.

Sue Sitki, a secretary at St. John's Hospital in Springfield and mother of three, has felt compelled to write "since scribbling in my diary about marrying Elvis Presley at age seven." Three of her plays have been produced: *Skydiving, Maura's Wedding* and *Dryspell*. She also sells her handcrafted jewelry at art fairs.

Debra Nickelson Smith has directed plays at theaters in Springfield and at the University of Illinois, and has taught English, composition, speech and theater at Lincoln Land College and Springfield College. Her plays have been performed onstage, and she has written articles for *Illinois Times* and the *State Journal-Register*.

Hilda Beltran Wagner is a teacher at Webster Academy, an alternative high school in Springfield, and a former Peace Corps volunteer who lived in Poland for two years. She has a master of fine arts degree from the University of Michigan. Her work has appeared in *Carolina Quarterly, Nebraska Quarterly* and *The Sun*.

Celia Wesle is retired from the Illinois State Board of Education, where she served as a consultant to school administrators and advised on women's equality issues in the schools. She has been poetry editor of a literary journal at the University of Wisconsin-Milwaukee, and has been published in the journals *Listening to Silence* and *Cheshire*.

Photos: Top row, from left, Sue, Jane, Celia. Row 2: Hilda, Martha, Maria. Row 3: Rosie, Debra, Nancy.

Afterword

Brainchild
a web, a circle, a center, a community,
women writers, sisters, a place, feeling
welcome, creative energy, open, where writing
is women's work, accepted, encouraged, critiqued

the writer
alone, blank paper, tools for writing, words,
brain, blood, bones, spirit, a unique view, a page
of words, this could be the end of it; instead,

the writer and Brainchild
with a little fear, a little excitement,
pages come with you to a meeting, and after all
the talking about life, our lives, the world around us,
amid a motley assortment of munchies, the readings begin,
soon it is your turn, you say you can't write, you say all sorts
of things are wrong with what you have written, but you'd
better read it anyway, they want you to, they want to hear you,
they are going to listen, you start to read, you hear your own voice,
your own words, they don't sound so bad, or maybe some of them do
but you can fix them, you know they understand, they are discussing
the issues around what you said, they tell you the parts they like
especially, where it needs fixing, where they got lost, and no one
laughed, no one said that's not writing, your reality becomes
larger, more real, being a writer; being in Brainchild;
in this way, you can see what might happen.

— Kate Kanaley Miller